Lucy Ryder Richardson

100
Midcentury
Chairs

and their stories

Contents

Introduction

You cannot be half-hearted when designing a chair. It has to be comfortable, resilient, play its part in a room, work as a group or stack as high as technically possible. Often an arduous journey, architect Ludwig Mies van der Rohe described the "Endless possibilities and many problems" of the design process, adding, "It is almost easier to build a skyscraper than a chair." [1]

"The chair does not exist. The good chair is a task one is never completely done with." [2]

Hans J. Wegner

"Chair love" for passionate followers of midcentury modern equates to car love in automobile enthusiasts. You will hear collectors talk about the patina of the wood, the curve of the seat, the sublime joinery, the dowels. They will ask for proof of original screws, sticker and production number, and are prone to wax lyrical about particular favourites over dinner, the way a vintage car fan enthuses over early Jaguars, Ferraris or Aston Martins.

People get really het up about chairs. When Marcel Breuer designed his first Clubsessel B3 in 1925, inspired by his trusty Adler bicycle, it got a mixed reaction. The artist Wassily Kandinsky may have been in awe of the chair with its bandaged tubular steel that was eventually named after him, but others were furious. "The Wassily was so new people jumped on it in exhibitions in order to destroy it. They thought the world was going to end with this furniture," Breuer said. [3]

Although Breuer quickly rose through the ranks at the Bauhaus from youngest student to teacher, life as a designer was not plain sailing. With designs evolving as rapidly as they did during the twentieth century, rights of design ownership often became blurred. He was taken to court, and lost a patent lawsuit, to Dutch designer Mart Stam, inventor of the world's first metal cantilevered chair. When he encountered a similar problem with Alvar Aalto's producer Artek some years later over the design of his Long Chair (page 26), he won. While it was true that Breuer had used plywood in a similar way to the Finnish designer, Aalto had clearly been inspired by Breuer from the outset. He had the Wassily chair in his office and was ordering Breuer's chairs for his buildings before he ever started designing furniture himself.

Not giving credit where credit is due can stir up trouble, as Charles and Ray Eames discovered when a group of creatives from the Eames studio walked out of "The Shop" in Venice Beach and into the arms of the Eameses' college friend turned producer, Florence Knoll. Supreme talents like Harry Bertoia and Eero Saarinen will only stay shackled to someone else's brand name for so long before it starts to irk, no matter how friendly and inspiring a boss you are. But working for yourself during the midcentury often put designers at a disadvantage too. While British designers often went for a gentleman's agreement, enabling relationships like Robin Day and Hille or Ernest Race and J.W. Noel Jordan to flourish, most US design firms required new designer employees to sign away all patentable rights for a dollar. Refuse to sign and you would be frozen out of the job.

There was another problem on both sides of the pond. Unscrupulous manufacturers would swoop in the minute a design garnered recognition. Even the mild-mannered, buttermilk drinking Hans J. Wegner was furious at the speed he was copied according to his daughter. Both Peter Ghyczy and Norman Cherner had producers who told them their chairs were too expensive to produce and then went on to manufacture them behind their backs.

We have an intimate connection with chairs. They surround our bodies, they receive our imprint, they leave memories and are often passed down from family member to family member. No wonder chairs can bring out the best and worst in people. They are also the quickest way to connect with the public, which is why so many architects design them. "Furniture and especially chairs interest me because it is a piece of architecture on the human scale. That's why architects design furniture – to design a piece of furniture you can hold in your hand," said Charles Eames, who saw his role as a designer to be like "a good host anticipating the needs of his guest". [4] The first to realize television was the best way to get a chair sold across America, the Eameses made the public a large part of the story when they launched their 670 Lounge Chair on national TV. The savvy Danish designer Arne Jacobsen worked out that a chair could serve as a business card for your practice, as well as garner sales in the lean years between builds. He would often call up the press just before a new model was about to emerge from his practice in order to get people excited.

RIGHT: Hjorth Chair, Axel Einar Hjorth, 1928.

During the midcentury, architects found they could send a message to the world with a mass-produced chair much more quickly than they could convey it in a building. When Jorge Ferrari-Hardoy, Juan Kurchan and Antonio Bonet made their name with the Butterfly Chair (page 30) in the thirties, they heralded the need for a more relaxed home as much as Chanel wearing trousers on the beach at Deauville demanded a more casual fashion code. Gaetano Pesce's UP5 Donna (page 188) was one man's call for the unchaining of women, just as Betty Friedan's celebrated book *The Feminine Mystique* delivered the same message from the woman's perspective. Meanwhile, the Blow chair by Jonathan De Pas, Donato D'Urbino, Paolo Lomazzi and Carla Scolari represented a break from tradition and from their parents' generation, inviting people to buy throwaway furniture with no history attached to it.

All the while these designers were at the centre of the story that would become midcentury modern, creating another piece of the patchwork, part of the timeline of action and reaction, with each story a contribution to the evolution of chair design. Aalto sitting with the Wassily chair in front of his desk and ordering Breuer's early designs for his buildings from the Thonet catalogue. Designers and retailers tripping to the Paimio tuberculosis sanatorium to see what all the fuss was about and then coming back with ideas of their own. The fostering of America's greatest talents Saarinen, Bertoia and the Eameses at Cranbrook Academy that ignited a revolution in design. The Hilles spotting Eames work in New York and deciding to hire their own Eames – the yet to be discovered Robin Day. The Pirelli rubber company seeing the work of Marco Zanuso at MOMA and architect Franco Albini's "gommapiuma" designs at the 1936 Milan Triennale before joining the dots to create a revolution in upholstery. Designers including

Mogens Koch, Ferrari-Hardoy, Kurchan and Bonet, Jens Risom and Hvidt & Mølgaard working out clever ways to fold or knock down their furniture so it could be exported and stored more easily for retail, which would lead to the birth of IKEA. The chair is not just an aesthetically pleasing and functional piece of design; it holds in its intricate construct an elaborate story, which, when woven with another story, becomes a taste of the times seen through the eyes of the people who design, sell and collect the chairs.

So what exactly is midcentury and midcentury modern?

It is hard to define the timeline of midcentury modern. Some limit the era to between 1947 and 1957, some 1950 to 1965. Although author Cara Greenberg first coined the phrase when she wrote the book *Mid-century Modern: Furniture of the 1950s* in 1984, writers tend to shape the term to different dates depending on which area of architecture and design they are describing. At our midcentury shows we take in everything from the thirties to the seventies because we believe that midcentury in chair terms starts in the early thirties with Alvar Aalto's organic cantilever (page 10) and ends in the early seventies with Frank Gehry's design that wrapped up Gerrit Rietveld's angular Zig Zag (page 17) and Verner Panton's sinuous Panton (page 158) into a sustainable cardboard Wiggle (page 196). In acknowledging what goes before and what comes after you are able to bookend the midcentury era and put it into context.

Our story starts in the lead up to the Second World War, as Scandinavian designers moved away from the "machine" ethos of the Bauhaus and took chair design to a place where nature would dominate again. As war started and Jewish designers were forced to find safe havens in places like Sweden, the UK and US, a spanner was thrown into the works. Supplies of materials like wood and canvas were diverted to the war effort, designers were forced to adapt to any material they could lay their hands on, reacting and changing to their environment like chameleons moving from rock to leaf.

The design profession ebbs and flows, and thrives on uncertainty better than most. Take away metal and the artist will head for the woods – or the bamboo grove in the case of Charlotte Perriand. Challenged by a shortage of cord or rope they might use raffia, paper or cellophane for a woven seat. Take away fabric and padding and the designer will look for alternatives. Bruno Mathsson and Jens Risom were among a number of designers who found new ways to upholster: Mathsson used saddle webbing and Risom used the parachute straps left over from war. Constraint, one of Charles Eames' favourite words, gave designers a tighter remit, thereby encouraging ingenuity and innovation to thrive.

What we now call "repurposing" or more crudely "upcycling" was at its height after the Second World War as designers looked at ways to use redundant machinery and materials. Wood cuts were put back into making jigs or prototypes, or could be used to power a furnace. Eero Saarinen and the Eameses avoided waste by upholstering any chairs that cracked during manufacturing. Finn Juhl stripped chairs back to the bare bones of upholstery without losing their luxurious look. As war cut the umbilical cord with their parents' generation, midcentury designers pushed technology forward, creating affordable design using materials employed in wartime – fibreglass, metal and plywood – in exciting and transformative new ways.

RIGHT: MR20, Mies Van Der Rohe, 1927.

Scandinavians Alvar Aalto, Bruno Mathsson, Finn Juhl and Grete Jalk pushed form to the limit, softening the architectural shapes of Kaare Klint, Le Corbusier and Mies van der Rohe to form a new organic Modernism. Post-war creatives looked to serve society on a much deeper level with "Good Design" as extolled by MOMA, New York's Museum of Modern Art, which highlighted a new informal way of living that freed up space in the room. Post Second World War designers proved you could make something durable and long-lasting for less money, a notion that might be hard to believe today when items are deliberately given a "lifespan" to make you go back and buy replacements. Design was seen as an evolutionary rather than a revolutionary practice. "Innovate as a last resort. More horrors are done in the name of innovation than any other," said Charles Eames.[5]

The years between the thirties and the middle of the seventies are essential to the evolution of chair design as this is when all the masters of the modern look were actively creating. News of exciting new furniture and ways of building spread across the world via two magazines in particular, Gio Ponti's *Domus* in Italy and John Entenza's *Arts & Architecture* in America, causing a cross-pollination between American and European designers as showcased in Denmark's Cabinetmakers' Guild exhibitions, Milan's Triennales and MOMA's Low-Cost competitions. Those returning from the war needed quick fix housing and the more savvy developers reacted to this need. GIs forced to bunk down with parents in New York were soon able to head to what is seen now as the archetype for postwar suburbs, the experimental new Levittown on Long Island to a built-in kitchen, weekly mowed lawn and picket-fenced quiet life. As creative families looked to a more open plan way of living, John Entenza suggested a case study of prefab houses to curb the same housing problem in California and American designers like the Eameses and Edward Wormley created pieces for this new modern lifestyle that would float in these houses as Hans J. Wegner, Arne Jacobsen and Poul Kjærholm were doing in Scandinavia.

As you research the stories and hear who inspired whom, you wonder where midcentury design would be without lessons learned from past masters like William Morris of the Arts and Crafts movement or the precursor to the Bauhaus, Josef Hoffmann, and the strong graphics of his Wiener Werkstätte. What if René Herbst had never experimented with tubular steel, rubber strapping, Bakelite and plastic as a countermovement to Art Deco? Or if Cubist painters had not broken up form into its most abstract composition and inspired furniture makers like Finn Juhl?

Take the inventor of the cantilever chair Mart Stam out of the grand Modernist puzzle and a whole new furniture blueprint might emerge. Go even further back past Thomas Chippendale, who inspired so many of the Danish masters, to the throne-like wooden chairs used by Chinese merchants, past the folding wooden chairs marauding Vikings carried on their backs from camp to camp for their masters, and even further back to the Egyptian thrones and stools that inspired Danish midcentury designers.

Today's furniture designers owe their creative backbone to the midcentury masters who became experts of ply and supernovas of steel, who studied the history of chair design, the human body and ergonomics, who built new jigs and pushed new ways of working with wood to the limit, learned to galvanize, to temper foam and to mould plastic. Carefully dissect the stories and archive photos, and the evolution of chairs starts to emerge. "Eventually everything connects – people, ideas, objects... the quality of the connections is the key to quality per se," said Charles Eames. "I don't believe in this 'gifted few' concept, just in people doing things they are really interested in doing. They have a way of getting good at whatever it is". [6]

As former dealers, now organizers of various vintage and modern collectors' shows, Petra Curtis and I have read our fair share of chair books. We are passionate enough about midcentury design to write one on Hans J. Wegner, Arne Jacobsen or the Eameses alone. Forced to pick and choose for this book, we have steered clear of prototypes you will rarely spot outside a museum in order to concentrate on pieces you can readily buy vintage or new. We wanted to create something we ourselves would find useful when visiting shows and auctions. A book that illustrates the evolution of midcentury chair design clearly. One that would spark up the imagination and satisfy the human need for stories. Rather than cluster chairs together in designer chapters, we have presented them chronologically in order to see which chair followed which up the evolutionary chair chain – although there will be some points of conjecture. Having researched each chair to the nth degree, going back and forth to get quotes from the partners, children and grandchildren of the designers, we wondered what else might you, the reader, need in your exploration of this fascinating era? So we gave our book an international directory of dealers that you can dip in and out of and use as inspiration when visiting dealers, fairs and auction houses.

We hope this new-found knowledge of the love, passion and hard graft that goes into each of these one hundred midcentury chairs (we could have written about a thousand) will not only be essential reading for all midcentury fans, but will also inform people who eye up copies that you cannot possibly get good value for money with a Jacobsen or Juhl "style" chair.

Would you pay for a counterfeit of a song you liked with a substitute performer? Or a copy of a film with a totally different lead actor? People who buy imitations will find the buzz short-lived as they realize that they have sacrificed quality to get their midcentury hit. Benjamin Cherner, Norman Cherner's son, says, "If Cherner, Herman Miller or Knoll were to produce their iconic pieces in a way that wasn't absolutely perfect, if for some reason the quality went down, that would be it for the brand. A Cherner chair sells for over $1000 now, but 99 per cent of the people we sell to wouldn't think of buying a knock-off. It's an investment. They know that if you buy the real thing, with a certificate of authenticity, and the high level of fit and finish, it is valuable and is never going to lose its value." As we

go to press, the good news for designers and midcentury dealers is that new laws are being brought in to stop companies from copying furniture down to the last dowel.

"Never let the blood show," said Charles Eames. But it is there, locked into the curve of the wood or the weave of the paper cord. The designer might hide quite how challenging the process of creating a chair has been, and producers may bend the story a bit to suit their PR, but as with a favourite work of art, where the story brings the brushstrokes alive, those of us who love chairs want to know the minutiae of our favourite designs' creation. Our midcentury chair is not simply something to sit on, polish or show proudly to our friends. An essential part of design history's elaborate tapestry, it has a story as rich as the patina left by the people who sit in it.

Please note

The order of the title on each page is: Chair name, Original number where known, Designer, Original Producer/maker, Date of design. In our desire to see the history of midcentury chairs in chronological order we have included the original producer and original design year (not production date). We appreciate that there is often controversy surrounding this subject.

Oh, and midcentury has no hyphen in our book as we think it looks prettier that way. We do hope you enjoy this book. Thanks for taking the time to read it.

Lucy Ryder Richardson
Founding Partner, Midcentury Modern and
The Modern Marketplace www.modernshows.com

1 Paimio Armchair 41, Alvar Aalto

Are there ever times in history where you wonder, if I took that moment out what would the world have looked like? That moment in the midcentury modern story is Paimio. It is where our story starts. Paimio was a sanatorium. It was also a chair. A very special kind of chair that inspired Charles Eames and Eero Saarinen to take up bentwood as a technique after they visited Alvar Aalto's architectural masterpiece and were blown away by the furniture inside.

Before the widespread use of antibiotics during the Second World War the only known cure for tuberculosis, otherwise known as "the white plague", was rest, clean air and sunshine; therapy that often took a couple of years. So when king of the curve, architect Alvar Aalto won the commission to design a tuberculosis hospital in Paimio, south-west Finland – built between 1930 and 1932 and inaugurated in 1933 – he wanted the building and its furniture to be as much a contributor to the healing process as the treatment from its doctors and nurses.

With Aalto's "medical instrument" came a huge roof terrace where patients would be taken in their beds as part of their daily routine to enjoy fresh air and views of the forest. A south-facing balcony was added to the end of each floor to give the bedridden as much sunlight as possible. Paths with water features wound around the grounds to encourage able patients to take walks. With his wife Aino he designed lighting fixtures and clocks, even door handles that would not catch on the doctors' lab-coat sleeves as they were prone to do.

By using wood he gave the cantilever many of his contemporaries were working on in metal, a less clinical look. With Otto Korhonen of the Oy Huonekalu-ja Rakennustyötehdas AB furniture factory he was able to develop a new construction process for laminated birch or beech that made furniture more flexible.

Designed to sit the tuberculosis patient up at just the right angle to help them breathe, the Paimio Armchair features two loops of beech (later birch) fused together to form arms, legs and floor runners and a slither of layered and laminated wood balancing delicately in the middle. Aalto had Korhonen use heat and pressure to loop the layers of glued veneer into scrolls top and bottom to strengthen the places that generally get more wear and tear. These acted like springs, allowing a certain bounce. "Though buoyant as a spring cushion, the seat back is virtually unbreakable," [7] Aalto said at the time.

Proof that Aalto pushed his lamination to the limit, a year later backrest slits were introduced to the design to release the stress from pressing. With the slits, the curve became even more flexible, which also made it easier to attach the handrails. Indeed, without the slits the chair could end up crooked, according to Korhonen's great-grandson Joonas who still runs Artek's A-factory (the name of the Oy Huonekalu-ja factory arm that now works with Artek as a subsidiary of Vitra). Whichever Paimio you prefer, you cannot help but marvel at Aalto's sculptural tour de force that inspired some of the greatest designers of the twentieth century.

1931

2 Armchair 31, Alvar Aalto, Oy Huonekalu-ja Rakennustyötehdas AB

In 1933, architectural critic Philip Morton Shand contacted Alvar Aalto to ask if he and his business partner Geoffrey Boumphrey could become the distributor for the Finnish master in the UK. Morton Shand had already struck up a friendship with Aalto and organized an exhibition of his work at Fortnum & Mason in November 1933, and he was keen to keep the momentum up. Aalto agreed; a London shop and distribution company was set up and Finmar soon became a temple to Scandinavian design. Boxy brown leather armchairs and three-piece suites were banished to the attic as Finmar brought Scandinavia's light, bright and revolutionary concept for a new way of living to the UK. No one in Britain had seen such curvilinear pieces nor such extraordinary wood veneers until this point. Chairs hung from the walls of the Kingly Street shop. Clouds of delicately pleated Le Klint paper lanterns floated above dynamic pieces by Aalto, Arne Jacobsen, Hans Wegner and Børge Mogensen.

The 31 chair combines Scandinavian tradition with the cantilevered work of Mart Stam and the work of Marcel Breuer at the Bauhaus. Designed for the Paimio Sanatorium in 1931–2 and sold by Finmar from 1935, the chair in the photograph was bought around the time of a design-savvy man's marriage to a North London widow during the war. Little did she know of its worth, until years later when her architect grandson spotted its familiar cantilevered shape in her attic and carefully peeled off layers of paint to find the masterpiece in Karelian birch underneath. This cantilevered chair was one of many designs

that Morton Shand would have originally seen at Paimio in the patients' rooms when he and Isokon's Jack Pritchard were taken on a personal tour led by Aalto.

> **"There is a degree of honesty and solidity about Finnish design that gives it its value. Some of the furniture is being sold now 70 years later and looks as contemporary now as it did then. They are justifiably proud of their international icons."** [8]
>
> Tom Dixon

Savvy collectors will look for Karelian birch chairs like the one pictured where the pattern to the veneer is much more intricate. Even though the Karelian birch veneer was used post war at the Hedemora factory in Sweden, and since then in special Artek editions, many are rare examples from the pre-war era. The young fiancé was lucky to have got this particular chair. Oy Huonekalu-ja Rakennustyötehdas AB in Turku, the original factory working for Aalto, where Artek's Aalto collection has been produced under the name A-factory since 2014, was unable to keep up with demand and many orders had to be put on hold. It was after Morton Shand's coaxing that Aalto set up Artek to cope with the overspill – and Artek, with Aalto, became huge players in the design world.

1931-2

3 Folding Chair, MK99200, Mogens Koch

Mogens S. Koch, the son of the Danish designer of the same name, remembers his father pulling his Folding Chair, with its original canvas armrests, away from the fire at home for fear it would go up in flames. One of four prototypes the Koch family were forced to keep because no one would buy them, this chair was so ahead of its time that when fellow designer Børge Mogensen asked his manufacturer Andreas Graversen of Fredericia Møbelfabrik to put the folding chair into production in the fifties, Graversen rather scathingly replied that he would not be producing furniture made from what he called "sticks".

First unveiled at a church interiors competition in 1932, with wooden balls as detailing, Koch's Folding Chair was influenced by Kaare Klint's favourite book, *Safari: A Saga of the African Blue*. Klint was Koch's teacher at the Royal Academy of Fine Arts in Copenhagen, and loved telling his students the story of American cinematographer Martin Johnson's three-year African adventure with his wife in the twenties. Koch, who later worked for him, particularly liked the image of the Johnsons sitting on the canvas and wood folding chairs of British officers outside their two-man tent. Klint also showed his students a folding stool he had designed in class with a student, based on the officer's chair and using aircraft propeller shafts as inspiration for the leg design. The Propeller Stool folded vertically and could be converted from stool into side table with the simple addition of a wooden tray. Koch wanted to make his chair equally easy to store and transport, without losing its sophistication. He used brass rings on all four legs to create a smooth closing movement and leather to take it up a notch. Like the officer's chairs the Johnsons used in the wild, the Folding Chair stabilizes itself automatically when a person sits on it.

Koch refused to give up on his ingenious prototype, which, by using brass and elegant woods like beech and mahogany, offered a refined alternative to earlier safari and director's chairs. He introduced a more simplified version, without the ball detailing, at Copenhagen's annual Cabinetmakers' Guild Exhibition in 1935 with extended arms that he was forced to whittle and attach himself after his carpenter made the "sticks" too short. Ironically a Spanish firm who tried to copy the Folding Chair later chose this particular "extended" prototype and copies from this run have become a bit of a joke amongst Danish collectors.

No producer had the confidence to take the chair under its wing until designer Axel Thygesen from Interna happened upon Koch's chair in an old *Dansk Kunsthåndværk* (Danish Craft) journal. Recommissioned with leather arms as part of a collection that included a smaller Grandchild Chair created for Axel Thygesen's daughter Michaela, the collection was displayed at Købestævnet, a manufacturers' exhibition, in 1950.

1932

4 Deck Chair, Kaare Klint, Rud. Rasmussen

When he put the human at the very centre of both his and his students' studies, Klaare Klint instigated a new way of thinking about furniture. He researched designs based on proportions adapted to the human body and extolled the use of the best and most local materials, paving the way for Danish design internationally. His studies resulted in a set of standardized measurements that are still used by designers today. Often referred to as the godfather of Danish design, Klint taught many of the design greats at the furniture school he headed up within the Royal Academy of Fine Arts in Copenhagen after it was founded in 1924. Stripping everything back to its function, including a Thomas Chippendale chair, his method of

deconstructing and creating furniture in front of students including Grete Jalk and Børge Mogensen gave them a greater understanding of materials and construction.

The idea of a folding chair is not a new one. Unearthed from archaeological digs in Egypt, Greece, Italy, the Far East and Scandinavia, Vikings carried them on their backs and Marcel Breuer and Gustav Hassenpflug played with folding chairs at the Bauhaus. Klint wanted to develop a more rational folding method than he had seen with cruise ship chairs, but while his use of teak enabled the user to take his 1933 Deck Chair inside and out, and an ingenious folding mechanism incorporating Klint's favourite brass fittings ensured it could be stowed away in a neater way with its fellow lounge chairs in winter, the rattan involved in the seat would never have survived aboard a ship.

Savvy collectors look for a removable upholstered pillow and a thin padded mat that were part of the original design. The mat should be doubled back after the leg rest has been made to slide back under the chair with its folding stand. Klint made it just the right thickness to be comfortable when lying down and realized that doubling the mat when sitting up added the extra comfort needed to allow for adjusting your weight from lying down to sitting up. Testament to its good design, little has changed in the look of garden lounge chairs today. While "luxury teak lounger" companies have replaced the cane with teak bars, they have never quite been able to improve on Klint's handmade design available in both teak and oak, and now only made to order by Rud. Rasmussen's craftsmen. Early Deck Chairs are rare and highly collectable.

1933

Zig Zag Chair, Gerrit Rietveld, Metz & Co.

In 1918–19 a Dutch architect and interior designer carefully constructed a wooden armchair using thirteen square battens, two rectangular armrests and two plank-style panels to create a new piece of furniture with intersecting planes that was all about sculptural functionality: a lesson in geometry, it was an armchair in its purest form. Painted in Mondrian colours in 1924, the Red and Blue Chair became a visual manifesto for the De Stijl movement and, as a technically challenging piece, has become an exercise for architects, many of whom try to make their own.

However it was Gerrit Rietveld's Zig Zag Chair that had the greatest impact on midcentury designers themselves – including Verner Panton, who was influenced by Rietveld's Z structure and the counterbalancing of weights in the way he designed his S-shaped Panton Chair (page 158). Rietveld called it a "construction joke" but his chair is as serious a piece of design history as his Red and Blue Chair. To look at the Zig Zag Chair you would think it would collapse as soon as any weight was placed on it. However, the movement of a human's weight through the carefully constructed structure of balance and counterbalance, the dovetail joints between the seat and back, reinforcements with nuts and screws, strengthening wooden wedges placed in the corners and a longer bottom "zag" all add to the magic architectural formula that keeps it upright when a person sits on it.

Excited by Mart Stam's experiments with the cantilever in 1926 and the brothers Heinz and Bodo Raschs's Sitzgeiststuhl (Sitting Spirit Chair) of 1927, Rietveld initially tried bending fibreboard over steel in a zigzag pattern in 1932, but the fibre cracked. He then tried screwing bits of metal and wood together. After experiments with both wood and metal in 1932, it would take another two years for Rietveld to create the commercial, stable, stackable 18 millimetre (³/₄ inch) thick solid elm version of the Zig Zag Chair you see here. Designed in 1934, it went into production for Amsterdam department store Metz & Co. in 1935. The shop had its own wood manufacturing workshops where pieces could quickly be made up as orders proved popular in the store. Rietveld later brought out a matching table, armchair and children's high chair. Now produced by Italian production house Cassina, the Zig Zag Chair makes a dramatic side table as well.

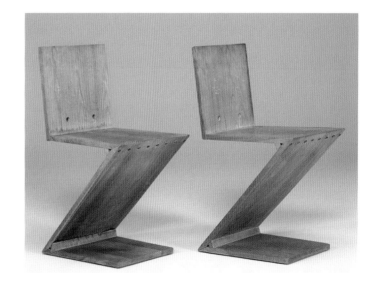

6 Eva Chair, T101, Bruno Mathsson, Firma Karl Mathsson

On his return to the Museum of Modern Art in the seventies, the *New York Times* put a splash on the front page saying, "Bruno is back". [9] This testament to America's love for the Swedish designer stretched back three decades to when Edgar Kaufmann jr, the twenty year old design department manager at MOMA, spotted Mathsson's chairs in the Swedish Pavilion of the Paris Expo of 1937 and bought a job lot for the museum's new extension.

Mathsson perfected the art of sitting by studying the shape his body made when he fell back into a snowdrift at different angles, and made numerous drawings that document this fact. He taught himself how to laminate wood in water, rather than steam, so that it bent slowly and never came apart, which makes his furniture more hard-wearing than most. What would evolve into the Eva Chair originally had a squarer bentwood leg with a crossbar at the back and the front, and was initially called the Working Chair. The later one from 1941 has legs that taper and looks like a cat ready to pounce.

Alvar Aalto was working with bentwood around the same time as Bruno Mathsson, and Mart Stam had already criss-crossed fabric on one of his versions of Model S33, the first cantilever chair of 1926. But Mathsson was the first to utilize the jute webbing used inside and underneath upholstered chairs and beds as a fabric for the main seat of chairs. When Mathsson first experimented with jute on his Grasshopper Chairs (1931) for the reception of his local hospital in Värnamo, Sweden, the chairs were considered so ugly by staff that they squirrelled them away from view, only to bring them out again when he became famous. Refusing to be put off by this rebuttal, Mathsson employed the straps again on his Vilstol and Eva Chairs. And when jute and hemp were no longer available during the war, he upholstered his furniture with paper saddle-girths, one of the fabrics used at the time to stop a saddle from slipping. He added a stuffed cushion of reindeer hair or a printed fabric from Svenskt Tenn designer Elsa Kullberg. Conceptually different from any other chair that had been created for export up until this point, Mathsson's Eva was ergonomic, feminine and supremely comfortable with its carved wood seat edges and bent laminated beech arms and legs.

Mathsson is often compared with Alvar Aalto, but after a journalist dared to suggest that some of Mathsson's chairs might impinge on Aalto's patents following the 1937 Paris exhibition, Mathsson wrote to the Swedish Society of Industrial Design saying, "I find it hard to understand why my chairs, which are the practical result of theoretical speculations about the mechanics of sitting, should be compared with or constitute an encroachment on Aalto's creations." [10] While Aalto's work may have been hugely inventive in its laminating technique, there was no ripping off on Mathsson's part. Rather the Swedish Mathsson and Finnish Aalto were beautifully inspired by each other. Aalto even used leather and jute cross-hatched strapping on his chairs at the latter end of the thirties and into the forties.

"The act of sitting comfortably is a skill, although it shouldn't be. Instead, the manufacture of seating should be carried out with such skill that the act of sitting in them becomes quite simple." [11]

Bruno Mathsson

1934

7 Chaise A, Xavier Pauchard, Tolix

Designers at the Bauhaus might have explored the many uses for sheet metal throughout the twenties and thirties, and Jean Prouvé made it an art form, but it was another Frenchman who took metal to the masses with a chair that has come to be known as "the 2CV of furniture". [12] This champion of ordinary folk with an extraordinary name saw its limitless possibilities while working as a zinc roofer with his father and grandfather. Xavier Pauchard went on to experiment with galvanization at the beginning of the 1900s and made his family's name by selling zinc-dipped metal products before he turned to selling furniture to businesses at rock bottom prices and became a very rich man off the back of it.

The Tolix name was trademarked in 1927 (with the 'x' at the end for Xavier) after Pauchard designed a pressed, folded and welded chair with an arched back and legs, round at the front and curved at the back, with a small flare to make it stackable, and other pieces of furniture went into production. The most popular of all Tolix chairs, the Chaise A was launched in 1934. A job lot made it aboard a ship called *Normandie*, although one wonders how long they lasted as the galvanizing process is not sea-salt proof. Tolix chairs filled the aisles of the 1937 Exposition Internationale des Arts et Techniques dans la Vie Moderne in Paris the year Communist Russia and Nazi Germany endeavoured to outdo each other in architectural brilliance. Leg stiffeners were added in 1938 (as seen here on this hand-stripped early Tolix). Cafes, factories, offices and hospitals all put in orders for Pauchard's chairs and bar stools in different colours. Contrary to popular belief, the plain metal chairs were not galvanized, like his metal products, instead lead was added to the paint to minimize corrosion – so be aware of the health hazards when stripping an old one. A new armchair A56 followed in 1956 as clients started demanding greater stackability. Tolix chairs were given to brasseries by breweries as incentives to get the owner to sign up to their brand of wine or beer in the fifties, and Xavier's son Jean tweaked Chaise C to enable cafes to stack twenty-five rather than ten of the chairs, by taking out the sides and lowering the back. He added a palm leaf motif to the Chaise A in 1960. [13] Sales went quiet when the brand lost ground to the plastic revolution in the sixties and, even though Chaise A was championed by Conran decades later, the company was threatened with bankruptcy in 2004.

> "Making space profitable, putting as many drinks as possible on the tables and optimizing the back and forth journeys of the waiters; turning cafe terraces into profitable business was the challenge of my family." [14]
>
> Xavier Pauchard

But there is a new excitement surrounding this democratic chair. You may have seen the Tolix A with its leaf motif popping up in a rainbow selection of colours outside eateries more recently. Snatching Tolix from the jaws of liquidation, financial manager Chantal Andriot took over in 2004 and the company now goes from strength to strength. With forty-five different colours and a choice of five separate varnish coatings, the Tolix A has returned as the ubiquitous cafe chair.

1934

8 Crate Chair, Gerrit Rietveld, Metz & Co.

When his Crate series was heavily criticized in 1935 Rietveld defended the construction in a feature entitled "Professional Decay" in the October issue of *Bouwkundig Weekblad* as a "free carpentry method which goes straight to the point, is strong and as innocent as the knitted brows of our craftsmen."

Rietveld was already experimenting with prefabricated concrete slabs and slotting together plywood, fibreboard and aluminium to create extraordinary experiments in geometry by 1927. This son of a Utrecht joiner, who worked in his father's workshop from the age of twelve, did not have the patience to spend years and years solving technical problems like his contemporary in Denmark, Kaare Klint. Although, like Klint, it was his dream to reduce chairs to the most simple equation, Rietveld also hoped to create quick, economical, knock-down furniture for the masses.

The publication of Rietveld's work in the journal *De Stijl* gave his career a considerable boost. Rietveld was rarely asked to make contributions to theoretical discussions in the journal – he was dyslexic, from a working-class background and not considered quite as highbrow as other members – but in 1919 Dutch artist and *De Stijl* founder Theo van Doesburg published two texts submitted by Rietveld to accompany illustrations of his Red and Blue Chair and baby's High Chair. Rietveld's contribution to the journal's jubilee issue in 1927 amounted to nothing more than a brief definition of what "true creation" is or ought to be.[15] Rietveld later said of the movement, "De Stijl had the intention of establishing a new style, while I was actually pursuing my personal study, but by chance this corresponded with the principles of De Stijl." [16] He broke with the De Stijl movement in 1928. Free to follow his functionalist dream without any constraints given to him by the group's occasional pretensions and unmoving principles, Rietveld started playing with the 15-centimetre (6-inch) wide firewood planks and brass screws that would become his Crate series.

Initially unvarnished and produced by Rietveld to order, a series was then sold – armchair, bookcase and small table – that were sold through Metz & Co. as "Weekend Furniture" from 1935. More designs soon followed, with Rietveld hoping they would be bought as kits for holiday homes: early IKEA if you like. But more often than not local customers commissioned the chairs so they could come and check on Rietveld's long-time carpenter Gerard van de Groenekan's progress and ask the carpenter to put the chair together for them at home. Italian production house Cassina later sold the series as both finished and DIY packs. To buy new go to Rietveld Originals, established by Rietveld's grandson Egbert Rietveld and his nephew Ries Seijler Rietveld in 2004 who, with designer Edward van Vliet, carefully studied old sketches and prototypes in order to revive a number of Rietveld classics.

1934

9 Standard Chair, No. 4, Jean Prouvé, Ateliers Jean Prouvé

Nothing excites us more than to hear the lengths a passionate dealer will go to for an artist's work. Eric Touchaleaume, the brains behind a large haul of Pierre Jeanneret's furniture from Le Corbusier's concrete city of Chandigarh in India, also spent the last decade scouring everywhere from a university refectory to war-torn Congo for the work of one of the greatest French designers of the twentieth century, the visionary engineer and architect Jean Prouvé, designer of the Standard Chair.

The son of an Art Nouveau artist, Prouvé was an exquisite metalworker. He created huge gates, store fronts, elevators, prefabricated houses and stunning pieces of furniture that are now considered works of art. He collaborated with great designers and artists including Charlotte Perriand and Alexander Calder. A devoted family man who flew planes and drove cars at full throttle, he enjoyed tinkering with his cars and listening to Bach at top volume.

Prouvé had a habit of balancing on the back legs of his chair while he came up with his ideas. He could see that thinner steel tubes worked at the front but realized he needed to engineer a back leg fit for purpose. So he invented one out of folded sheet metal which widened then tapered in a geometric style in order to pass weight down to the floor. While the use of sheet steel for a leg made a huge statement at the time, the slightly curved wood on the back and seat acted as a soft contrast. No doubt many inventive ideas sprang from the students who sat in the chairs which are now manufactured by Vitra – with a revised edition updated with a plastic seat and back by designer Hella Jongerius.

Created in 1934 for the university of his hometown, Nancy, the Standard came to life in the Ateliers Jean Prouvé, an innovative laboratory Prouvé founded in 1924. The experimental studio drew visits from architect Le Corbusier and created a huge back catalogue of work, much of which was patented, before Prouvé lost control to the French national aluminium company Studal in 1952. Prouvé left, bereft, saying, "I have nothing but my hands, my shocked brain and no financial reserves at all." [17] He was rarely out of work before his death in Nancy in 1984 and is still deeply respected by the art and architecture community.

Touchaleaume amassed more than 600 of Prouvé's chairs before turning to the prototype aluminium buildings Prouvé's team designed in France and exported to West Africa at the beginning of the fifties. As word spread around Congo's capital Brazzaville that Touchaleaume was looking for furniture from the former Air France building – which he was busy deconstructing to its flat-pack form – people started bringing pieces to him, risking shooting in the streets around Brazzaville.

Touchaleaume hired local bodyguards and had to negotiate for one of the buildings for six months while civil war was happening all around him. He eventually filled fifteen shipping containers with three of Prouvé's Maisons Tropicales and prime pieces of furniture, including many demountable versions of the famous Standard Chairs (with large screws in the sides). With his booty wrapped in banana leaves, Touchaleaume returned to France where eager collectors and gallerists were ready to bid for work from the most bankable designer/artist/engineer of all time.

1934

10 Long Chair, Marcel Breuer, Isokon Furniture Company

In March 1937 Bauhaus émigré László Moholy-Nagy designed a folding leaflet to advertise Marcel Breuer's Long Chair. Inside a man reclines, with arrows illustrating how he is supported, alongside the dramatic statement, "You have the amazing sensation of the Principle of Archimedes without being in Water!"[18] It is not known whether Moholy-Nagy, Walter Gropius, Breuer or Isokon founder Jack Pritchard came up with the line, or if it was a collaborative effort dreamed up in the designers' drinking hole Isobar at the Isokon flats, Wells Coates' minimalist urban-living experiment in north-west London. What we do know is that Alvar Aalto's experiments with cantilevered wood may never have existed without Breuer's cantilever chairs, or for that matter Mart Stam's (the Dutch designer who won the right to claim his was the first cantilever chair). Aalto first saw Breuer's chairs in a Thonet catalogue and installed a job lot in his early buildings. Years later Breuer was forced to return the compliment by bringing out a bent-ply daybed that would sit comfortably next to Aalto's Paimio designs (pages 10 and 12).

The Long Chair was a worthy rival to pieces British agent Finmar was importing from Aalto's company Artek in Finland at the time, and Breuer was less than happy when a legal battle ensued between Finmar and Isokon over similarities between the design and material of the Long Chair and Aalto's designs. Breuer had been reluctant to make a Long Chair in plywood in the first place, preferring to use his trademark aluminium. Isokon owner Jack 'Plywood' Pritchard was already working with a Baltic manufacturer and wanted to use the plywood and machinery he had access to. Having helped Breuer into the country and settled him at his landmark flats in Lawn Road, Pritchard was not going to take no for an answer and told Breuer the Brits were far too conventional for metal furniture (Ernest Race would later prove him wrong). Gropius suggested Breuer model the new bent-ply reclining chair on Breuer's own aluminium lounge chair design of 1933 to create a chair that could be mass produced. It was a far cry from the Hungarian born designer's B3 or his Wassily (a chair Aalto had in his own flat in Turku), but it did echo the adjoining arms and legs of the B35 armchair that he designed at the Bauhaus in 1928, which Aalto would have seen in the Thonet catalogue at some stage.

The Long Chair's seats were pre-bent at furniture manufacturer Luther's in Estonia. The chair frames, using 1.5-millimetre (^{1}/$_{16}$-inch) veneer salvaged from the packing cases sent from Luther's, were created in the Isokon workshop back in London and sold in birch or walnut (with or without upholstery created from a choice of Hairlok or Dunlopillo fillings). Over the next few years the now-patented Long Chair would undergo all kinds of tweaks and small changes in design to add to its strength and durability.

Breuer went on to design other pieces out of moulded plywood – his square table and dining table, nest of tables and stacking chair – before wood was diverted to the war effort and Isokon was forced to shut down in 1939, reopening in the early sixties. From tubular metal and fabric composer to organic Modernist, Breuer, with Aalto, was responsible for much of the groundwork that fed later experiments with plywood chairs by Harry Bertoia, Eero Saarinen and the Eameses, even though by the end of 1937 only eighty-nine Long Chairs had been sold when Breuer left for design-hungry America.

"Ten minutes in an Isokon Long Chair after a
meal is as good as any medicine." [19]

Jack Pritchard

1936

11 Lounge Chair 43, Alvar Aalto, Artek, 1937 (upholstered), 1947 (leather strapping and webbing)

The thirties saw a huge rise in leisure seating designed for reading, rehabilitation and hangovers brought on by the Jazz Age. Le Corbusier and Mies van der Rohe put flat roofs for sunbathing on their buildings and Bruno Mathsson and Alvar Aalto built homes around courtyards where outdoor relaxation could be made a priority.

Aalto wanted to bring out his own chair to lounge in but Marcel Breuer had already designed his Long Chair (page 26) for Isokon. Answering calls from buyers who wanted a more comfortable line than the Paimio chair offered, and perhaps also not wanting to be associated with Breuer's ply recliner, Aalto made his earliest 43 lounge chair for the Paris World's Fair padded (like he had done with his Tank chair a year before) and covered it in Marita Lybeck's "cloud" textile. Lybeck was known more as a ceramicist than a textile designer but her brother Nils-Gustav Hahl, one of Artek's co-founders, was keen for her to help with the piece.

The 43 lounge chair was presented in a conservatory next to Aalto's iconic tea trolley in the acclaimed Finnish Pavilion that Aalto built at the Paris World's Fair in 1937. The Finnish designer made his homeland's vast forests the main theme, with enormous photographs of wooded landscapes, tree trunks used as pillars and a curved building around a Finnish-style garden with Japanese touches. Mixing the supreme comfort of traditional lounge chairs with his bentwood mastery, the 43 chair opened Aalto's market up to people who may have overlooked his more minimal wooden seated chairs, although it was still sold in very small amounts.

Looking almost precarious from the side, you can see its elegance of form more in the criss-cross leather strapping version of Aalto's cantilevered laminated birch daybed pictured here. Brought out later with a fabric webbing option too, this 1947 version displayed an even lighter touch than Aalto would have achieved with a pure ply lounge chair. Note the pole balancing on the two legs at the back that looks like it might roll forward like a child's balancing toy. This elegant detail hides screw-fixings that come up from underneath to join the pole and stop the legs warping. From the side view you cannot see the other pole beneath the seat and so the recliner seems to float like Charlotte Perriand's reclining chairs. Now only made to order, the original 43s with leather strapping or fabric webbing are highly sought after, but one in the original upholstery from the late thirties would be an even rarer find.

1937

12 Butterfly Chair, 198, Jorge Ferrari-Hardoy, Juan Kurchan and Antonio Bonet, Artek-Pascoe

Effortless, minimal and loved by design junkies, beach bums, hipsters and students, it is hard to believe the Butterfly Chair, one of the most copied chairs of all time, was designed at a period in history when people still dressed in formal clothes. There was no way of sitting upright in it. The only option was to slouch.

When MOMA's design curator Edgar Kaufmann jr first spotted it in 1940 at the Third Salon de Artistas Decoradores in Buenos Aires, he had a feeling that West Coast Americans would eagerly snap up the lightweight chair, with its original tan leather sling, for its relaxed feel. Families were looking for reasonably thrifty furniture that would make a statement in their home and the Butterfly Chair embraced a new casual aesthetic with its leather hammock seat and zigzagging metal base. Kaufmann was so excited he ordered two: one for his parents' newly built Frank Lloyd Wright masterpiece Fallingwater and one for the Museum of Modern Art.

Also known as the BKF, the Hardoy, the Safari, the Sling and the Wing, it was originally designed for the office of three Argentine architects, Ferrari-Hardoy, Kurchan and Bonet, who had worked with Le Corbusier on a master plan for Buenos Aires. Collectively known as Grupo Austral, they put the first prototypes together as models before manufacturers Artek-Pascoe did pretty well

with it, sending royalties back to Argentina. However Knoll Associates thought it could do more to market the chair and acquired US production rights in 1947. Sadly the New York producer was unable to stem the flow of unauthorized copies in cheaper fabrics. It filed a claim for copyright infringement. But as much as it did not look like the original chair used by officers in the British Army, it had been inspired by a folding principle, that was patented in wood in 1877 by British engineer Joseph Beverley Fenby. The defence called it derivative.

Unable to compete on pricing and unwilling to sacrifice quality, Knoll was forced to drop the chair in 1950. More than five million copies of the Butterfly Chair were produced by various manufacturers during the fifties alone. Today, that number is hundreds of millions, with everyone from Walmart to IKEA having produced a Butterfly of their own at some stage. Originals are very collectable. Expect to pay a few thousand pounds for the original chair produced by Artek-Pascoe and around a thousand pounds for a Knoll Associates production. Although it could not stand up in court as an original design, the Butterfly Chair certainly proved to be the perfect two-fingered salute to the more angular looks popular in the thirties – and for that reason we salute it.

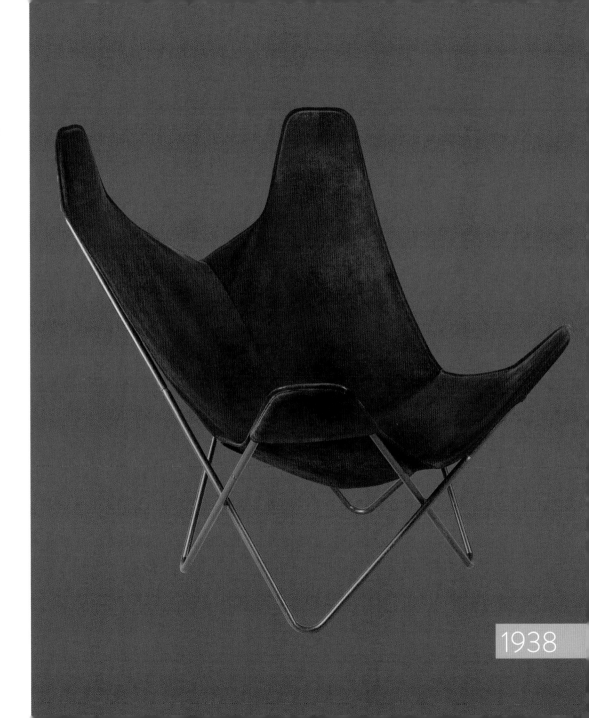

"The most successful chair of the twentieth century." [20]

Albert Pfeiffer

1938

13 Landi Chair, Hans Coray, P. & W. Blattmann Metallwarenfabrik

Ask any student starting out in the field of design and it is unlikely they would be able to date such a modern-looking piece to as far back as the thirties. And yet the lightweight Landi was created during the Second World War, just as designers were starting to look at the aviation industry for ideas. While wood was diverted to the war effort, aluminium became one of Switzerland's most important exports, able to withstand fire and rain and produced using the electricity, that was readily available through the country's hydroelectric power plants.

In 1938, Hans Coray, an artist and sculptor closely associated with Dada and the Concrete Art movement in Zurich, paid a visit to architect Hans Hofmann's office to show his assistant, ex-Bauhauser Hans Fischli, a sketch for display cases he had designed. Fischli hinted that rather than display cases, the management of the Swiss National Exhibition was on the hunt for a metal chair that could represent Switzerland around the world. So Coray went home and worked tirelessly on a chair made entirely of aluminium that could be vertically stacked, and headed back to see Fischli and Hofmann, who were so convinced by the design they were quick to show it to their employers.

The Swiss National Exhibition partnered Coray up with Blattmann, a metal company in Wädenswil that worked in conjunction with the Rorschach aluminium works. The resulting chair, inspired in part by a perforated chair Josef Hoffmann and Oswald Haerdtl had been playing with in 1929, was comfortable, stackable and weighed just three kilos (six pounds). Rendered as hard as steel through a special heat treatment involving chemicals that gave the surface of the chair a sheen that had never been seen before in metal, the Landi Chair must have looked like it had landed here from another planet. The curve of the edges and perforation of the seat and back that reduce the weight of the chair and allow rainwater to drain through were made possible with a 300-ton press.

Fifteen hundred aluminium, or "Swiss metal", chairs were installed in squares and parks around Zurich before the history of the classic chair was marked by alternating manufacturers, breaks in production and modifications to the original design. No caps were placed under the feet at first, but as it became a design classic and was brought inside, different types of plastic were played with before the black or white rubber caps we see today came into being. Collectors should be aware that a pre-1962 Landi will have ninety-one holes. Post 1962 the total changed to sixty, as in the archive photograph pictured. Post 1971 you might spot the name "2070 Spartana", which manufacturer Zanotta SpA marketed it under.

Coray's design went on to inspire a host of different designers including Gabriele Mucchi and Gerrit Rietveld who experimented with hole-punching metal. But none looked as modern as the Landi, which still looks as fresh as the day it was first produced, with Vitra returning to producing the chair with ninety-one holes as Coray originally intended.

1938

14 Sunbed, Aino Aalto, Artek

Architect and designer Aino Aalto was more than the wife of Alvar Aalto. Respected in her native country as a pioneer of Finnish design in her own right, she worked closely with her husband as Artek's first Artistic Director, on everything from textiles and lamps to glass and buildings. Preparer of plans and sketches, she was considered more gifted at drawing than Alvar. And while he played the charismatic bohemian, she was the down to earth practical one who brought a sense of calm and order to the office and ran all his affairs.

Aino assisted Alvar in designing fixtures and furniture for the Paimio tuberculosis sanatorium but is most recognized for her work at the Villa Mairea, a private villa in Noormarkku, Finland, built for Artek co-founder Maire and her husband Harry Gullichsen, who were ardent lovers of art. After some negotiation over interior walls, Alvar Aalto came up with a house based around a courtyard with a continuous 250 square metre (nearly 2,700 square foot) living space that adhered to the open-plan living of a traditional Finnish peasant house, but of course with a lot more space to house the Gullichsens' vast art collection.

Relaxation and taking time to enjoy the pine forest surrounding the house, and the blue sky above, was of paramount importance. Maire came from a family of hard-working sawmill and shipping owners who built an empire and had little time to enjoy it. Sunbeds were essential to the courtyard, tucked away from the unsettled world outside. In the years preceding Villa Mairea, Hitler was gearing up to invade the rest of the world. By 1939, the year Aino and Alvar finished the design, a world war had started.

Aino was given free rein to furnish the place with a considered Modernist mix of Alvar's furniture and her own custom-made designs. The Sunbed, with its wooden slats, wheels and handles that enabled you to move it around like a wheelbarrow, was originally hewn out of a conifer tree. Both Maire and Aino enjoyed lounging in white ones in their gardens, but it was also available in dark green, bright yellow, red and Alvar Aalto's favourite – a ship-tarred version in black.

The addition of wheels on a sunbed was nothing new. Thonet had played with them on his sinuous wicker sun loungers and Marcel Breuer and other members of the Bauhaus had experimented with them also, but, as always, Aino seemed to get her lines exactly right. Her design handwriting was a little stricter and less organic than Alvar's but her designs fulfilled their purpose beautifully without shouting for attention. While Alvar provided the dramatic lead roles, Aino filled in all the gaps to create perfect harmony in everything.

1939

15 Tokyo Chaise Longue, 522, Charlotte Perriand, Cassina

The story of how Charlotte Perriand got to work with Le Corbusier is written into Modernist folklore. After rejecting her with the phrase "We don't embroider cushions here", Le Corbusier saw the "bar under the roof" installation Perriand had re-created from her own aluminium, nickel-plated steel and glass loft space at Paris's 1927 Salon d'Automne and was forced to hire this gutsy lady immediately.

Perriand clearly relished her time with Le Corbusier, where she was integral to the furniture he and Pierre Jeanneret developed in collaboration with major artists and designers at the time, but she really came into her own when appointed as an advisor on industrial design to Japan's Ministry of Trade and Industry for a six-month placement that turned into two years. With limited production times and prohibition on materials, Perriand was forced to adapt very quickly for an exhibition she was commissioned to create. She wanted to show the Japanese, who were used to sitting on tatami floor mats rather than chairs, how it was possible to furnish every part of a Japanese home with furniture that could be exported to the rest of the world.

It was here she conceived her Tokyo Chaise Longue, a reinterpretation of the famous LC4 in tubular steel and leather or cowhide she created with Le Corbusier and Pierre Jeanneret in 1928, captured in the iconic 1929 photograph of Perriand lying back wearing her necklace made from ball bearings, her skirt hitched rather seductively for the time. With incredible craftspeople at her disposal she learned new techniques including lacquer and basket weave. She marvelled at how the Japanese bent bamboo using water or heat, and relished seeing rice straw and rice paper employed in a multitude of ways. Having already made her chaise longue in wood with a hammock of leather for the seat before arriving in Tokyo, Perriand set about adapting the design to take twelve strips of moulded bamboo, the curves at the edges adding strength to the chair as Alvar Aalto's Paimio Armchair (page 10) had done nine years earlier. Mr Yamaguchi, the Ministry of Agriculture director for the snowy mountainous region of Tohoku, showed her a mino – a straw raincoat worn by Japanese farmers – and it was from this that she commissioned a woven rice-straw fabric to drape over the bamboo, making it more comfortable and adding pattern and texture.

Perriand was forced to leave Japan after the country allied itself with Germany during the Second World War. An "undesirable alien" trapped by a naval blockade, she spent four more years in exile in Vietnam where she perfected pieces including her Ombra Tokyo Chair, developed from a single die-pressed piece of curved ply, as well as her Tokyo Chaise Longue, which is now produced by Cassina in bamboo, teak or beech. Charlotte Perriand, with her ideas about free-formed furniture designed to make "space sing", [21] put the human at the heart of her philosophies. At a time when women were excluded from design and architecture practices, Perriand excelled.

1940

16 Pelican Chair, Finn Juhl, Niels Vodder

When you consider that designers like Pierre Paulin and Olivier Mourgue were working twenty years after Finn Juhl designed this extraordinary upholstered chair, you realize that the design must have looked quite odd to the Danes, who saw it presented in 1940 with the equally unusual, equally stubby-legged Pelican Table. Upholstered chairs were not supposed to show their legs. They had larger cushions, more padded upholstery and were generally heavy and sprung. The Pelican had a thin layer of upholstery and a pine frame immaculately constructed by Niels Vodder from Juhl's simplistic drawings.

The architect wanted to create an upholstered solution for smaller, lighter apartments. Something that would sit easily with the abstract art of the day; a piece as sculptural as the work of Jean Arp, Henry Moore, Barbara Hepworth and Erik Thommesen. A chair that would not sacrifice comfort for ingenuity. An abstract body created to hold another body. But when Juhl's chair first appeared as a pair at the Copenhagen Cabinetmakers' Guild Exhibition the year Hitler invaded Denmark, rather than falling under Juhl's spell, the chairs were dismissed by his contemporaries as looking like a "couple of tired walruses" and "aesthetics in the worst possible sense of the word".[22]

Born in Copenhagen, Juhl graduated from the Royal Academy of Arts in 1934 and worked for the architect's practice Vilhelm Lauritzen before winning a prize for the design of his own home in 1942. He was already exhibiting furniture with master craftsman Niels Vodder at the annual Copenhagen Cabinetmakers' Guild Exhibition when he opened his design office – focusing on interiors and furniture – after commissions started to roll in off the back of his award-winning house.

With Hans J. Wegner and Arne Jacobsen, Juhl carved the way for Denmark's blaze of glory throughout interiors during the mid-twentieth century although he never became quite as famous as his contemporaries. While other designers looked to larger production, the father of Danish Modern stuck with smaller batches. Revolutionizing furniture was his goal more than money. By entering all of the furniture they made at Guild shows, where the emphasis was on the artisan rather than mass production, Juhl and Vodder could use expensive materials. Unconfined by the limitations of economy a manufacturer would place on them they were able to push furniture to the limits of possibility and wait for manufacturers to catch up.

The Pelican paved the way for fifties style, stripping upholstery back as Eero Saarinen would do with his Womb Chair (page 58) six years later. An outstanding, brilliant and comfortable piece that proved to be years ahead of its time, it was relaunched in 2001 and is now produced with a steel frame and foam shell.

"One cannot create happiness with beautiful objects, but one can spoil quite a lot of happiness with bad ones." [23]

Finn Juhl

1940

17 Poet Sofa, 705/FJ41, Finn Juhl, Niels Vodder

Architect, interior designer and furniture designer Finn Juhl was at the vanguard of Scandinavian modernism in the 1940s and 50s. Leading the revolt against the reigning heavy classical style, along with avant-garde Danish designers of the time – including Hans Wegner who very much respected his contemporary's work – Juhl believed you should design a home from the interiors and furniture out. And if the designs he created did not work in his own home they would be consigned to the wastepaper basket.

The Poet Sofa was one of the first pieces created for Kratvænget, the home in which Juhl lived from 1941 until his death in 1989. It did not get its name until 1950 when Jørgen Mogensen had a poet philosophising from it in his popular Politiken cartoon after seeing it at the home of Danish poet Frank Jæger and his wife Kirsten Vodder, daughter of the renowned cabinetmaker Niels Vodder, who worked with Finn Juhl for 22 years. She was given the sofa after the Cabinetmakers' Guild exhibition in 1945. It also made it to celluloid as the centrepiece in Erik Balling's 1959 Danish film *The Poet and the Little Mother* which was based on the cartoon. The film, starring Henning Moritzen, was entered into the 9th Berlin International Film Festival.

Juhl had not stripped his furniture right back to the bare bones at this stage, but still, the pared-down look of the Poet Sofa was almost too modern for people used to a more classical detailed style. No one would have seen anything like the sofa's legs at the time – which looked more like the top of broom handles and as with his Pelican Chair (page 38), these were oiled rather than varnished. The sofa was stuffed and very likely unsprung, according to Hans Henrik Sørensen, founding partner of Onecollection who now produce many of Juhl's chairs, "Today we use pocket springs inside the seat cushion but originally I do not think there were springs or latex." The fabric Juhl used on the outer layer was hand-woven and commissioned from weaver Dorris Nielsen.

While his home with its bare-boarded floors, bright colours and modern paintings would look quite beautiful now, it proved too much for the newspaper Politiken, which also pub-lished a cartoon with a lady standing in an open doorway pointing at a jumbled pile of chairs while inside the room is a Finn Juhl-style child's seat with a potty in it, and various other seats indicating different styles of repose, with the words: "The architect Finn Juhl has indicated that each of his chairs are designed for a specific sitting position. You can even tell him how you want to sit!"

1941

18 Risom Lounge Chair, 654W, Jens Risom, Hans Knoll Furniture

Jens Risom earned his place in a memorable line-up featuring Charles Eames, Eero Saarinen, George Nelson, Edward Wormley and Harry Bertoia, shot in 1961 for the centrefold of *Playboy* magazine, for changing the face of furniture to reflect a new modern America. He came to the US at the end of the thirties but it was not until a serendipitous meeting with Hans Knoll – the forward-thinking son of a German furniture manufacturer – in 1941 that he was able to turn his dreams into reality. Risom was looking for a visionary manufacturer to champion him in the US and Knoll was looking for a designer to create furniture with him locally in New York. Risom had a masterful way with shape and colour and a knack of distilling the mood. Knoll had worked on the factory floor with his manufacturer father Walter Knoll and had a deeply entrenched knowledge of the furniture business.

Both born on 8 May, but two years apart, they made a powerful team, producing Scandinavian modern design fit for the American palette; work that evolved from meticulous research they collated on a three-month tour around America where Knoll and Risom got a feel for what architects and interior designers might want to commission in the future, and at what price. The first collection Risom produced for Knoll in 1941 – cherry, birch and maple wood desks, cabinets, chairs and tables – reflected the new Scandinavian look and was popular, if unspectacular.

It was not until war disrupted supply lines that Risom's most famous designs were born. Drawing on the economy of Kaare Klint and the aesthetic sensibilities of Finns Alvar and Aino Aalto and Swede

Bruno Mathsson, whose work Risom had been exposed to when working as a young designer in Stockholm, Risom's Lounge Chair was honest in its display of form and function. Stripping the chair back to its skeleton structure, Risom worked with cedar offcuts for the structure and surplus parachute straps rejected by the military for the webbing while Knoll found small factories that had been spared from producing for war. Economy and lightness were crucial to the success of the 654W chair and together the pair discovered ways to make manufacturing and the assembly of knock-down pieces easier and more economical. What looks like steamed bentwood is anything but, with its simple sculpted and sliced-out shape achieved through mortise-and-tenon construction. After the war cedar was replaced with laminated beech, and the webbed seat and back were manufactured using a higher quality fabric or leather.

Debuting in 1943 (while Risom was at war designing quick-unzip camouflage jackets for Sherman tank crews and serving as a translator for General Patton) the 650 series was a huge success for its fresh new look, and became the go-to project furniture for American architects and interior designers throughout the war years. One of fifteen designs Risom produced for Knoll's twenty-five piece 650 collection, the 654W has since been employed in airports, company lounges and hotel lobbies, as well as the military mess. Look out for a "Vostra" label too. Knoll's father Walter Knoll sold Risom's 654W under this name in Germany from 1947, with an upholstered version selling from 1949.

1943

Grass-seated Chair, George Nakashima, Nakashima Studio

Designer George Nakashima called himself "a bit of a druid". Believing he was very much part of the process of giving a tree new life, he created beautifully handcrafted pieces with the utmost respect, as one of the main proponents of the American Crafts revival of the forties. Simple and comfortable, in spite of its primitive feel and angular shape, the Grass-seated Chair is one of the most popular and commercially successful of Nakashima's chairs, with its one steam-bent support that gently curves under the arms, predating Hans J. Wegner's Round Chair (page 78). Keeping spindles to a minimal six, Nakashima ensures you can see through the chair, with four flared legs joined by simple stretchers. The heaviest looking part is the walnut seat frame which Nakashima's wife Marion was given the task of weaving using baling twine they had lying around their homestead; seagrass was later used. And, while Mr Nakashima, as he was reverently addressed by both staff and customers, sought to explore the expression in each piece of wood, displaying knots and burls to maximum effect in larger pieces, the Grass-seated Chair sees husband and wife working on a simpler chair to give wood its second life.

Nakashima was born in America to Japanese parents. He studied architecture at MIT before spending a year living in France as a bohemian and travelling around North Africa and Japan. But nothing shaped Nakashima quite as much as a visit to India in 1936 where he volunteered to supervise the construction of the Sri Aurobindo ashram in Pondicherry. While working there, he had a revelation and was given the name Sundarananda, "One who delights in beauty", which set Nakashima on the path to discover *The Soul of a Tree*, a book he later wrote and published in 1981.

On his return to wartime America in 1942 Nakashima was one of many Japanese-American artisans confined to internment camps. He, his wife and daughter were sent to one in the Idaho desert where, fortuitously, he met a carpenter skilled in using traditional Japanese hand tools. Ever meticulous in his attention to detail, Nakashima never forgot his teachings when he left with his family to set up his own studio in New Hope, Pennsylvania, sponsored by Antonin Raymond, an architect he had worked for in Tokyo. Nakashima would travel the country just to find the right piece of wood. The more he showed his devotion to the material, the more he seemed to attract outstanding craftsmen, who wanted to learn from this master producing outstanding furniture as a silent protest against mass production.

Nakashima is one of the most sought-after designers by collectors today, including many celebrities. Nelson Rockefeller commissioned 200 pieces for his house in Pocantico Hills, New York, in 1973. Steve Jobs had new Nakashima pieces created by George's daughter Mira, who continues to stay faithful to her father's pursuit for perfection and has run the studio since her father died in 1990. The Grass-seated Chair is still in production, although the woven seagrass has recently been replaced by Danish cord for its strength and durability. Look for the Nakashima signature underneath the seat to be sure it comes from his studio.

"Work for him was a spiritual calling, a linking of his strength to a transcendental force, a surrender to the divine, a form of prayer."[24]

Mira Nakashima

1944

Pernilla 3, Bruno Mathsson, Firma Karl Mathsson

The Pernilla was named in honour of Pernilla Tunberger, a journalist who went by her first name alone as a writer for the Stockholm *Daily News*. She interviewed Mathsson at his home in 1943, the year the first Pernilla came into being, and they got along so well Mathsson did her the great compliment of naming his chair after her; a rare honour indeed.

Pernilla 1 was a short reclining version of the Eva Chair (page 18). Pernilla 2 had a footstool. Pernilla 3 merges both and is redolent of Marcel Breuer's Isokon Long Chair (page 26). Mathsson, a physical culturist who spent as much time sleeping in the open air as possible through the summer months, loved relaxing at home in the colder months in his own leather-webbed Pernilla 3, his arms resting on its laminated bentwood beech arms and solid birch underframe meeting bentwood legs tapering down to the floor.

Young Bruno learnt by experimenting with different types of wood in his father Karl Mathsson's workshop, which took up the basement and ground floor of their home in Värnamo. Once he knew the workings of a chair from the inside out, he set himself the task to strip it back to the bare minimum. Voracious in his reading, he borrowed boxes and boxes of books from Gustaf Munthe, the then curator at the Röhsska Arts and Crafts Museum in Gothenburg. His determination to learn about different styles of craftsmanship clearly impressed Munthe – so much so that he became a mentor and put on a one-man show for Mathsson in 1936.

Two years before the show, Mathsson designed his first Pernilla, although it was called the Reclining Chair back when Eva was called the Working Chair. Early Pernilla chairs had jute webbing but when jute and hemp were diverted to the war effort he experimented with the paper fabric used for saddle-girths as he had done with the Eva and upholstered his chairs using fabrics like sheepskin. By 1944, the year he designed the Pernilla 3, Mathsson was showing furniture in temporary interiors he created for the Karl Mathsson catalogues. Edgar Kaufmann jr, who loved the new stripped down Scandi-Style and had already furnished MOMA with Mathsson's chairs, made a special trip to see Mathsson in Sweden before arranging a tour of the US to enable him to showcase his work, put on exhibitions and meet up with architects and interior designers.

The most beady-eyed collectors will be on the look out for Karl Mathsson branding and the early paper-girth webbing, which is thinner than jute. There were also sheepskin and fabric versions made. Anything branded with Dux will be post 1978 and less collectable, but it should be cheaper than new and a beautiful bargain if you are buying vintage to enjoy at home rather than collect.

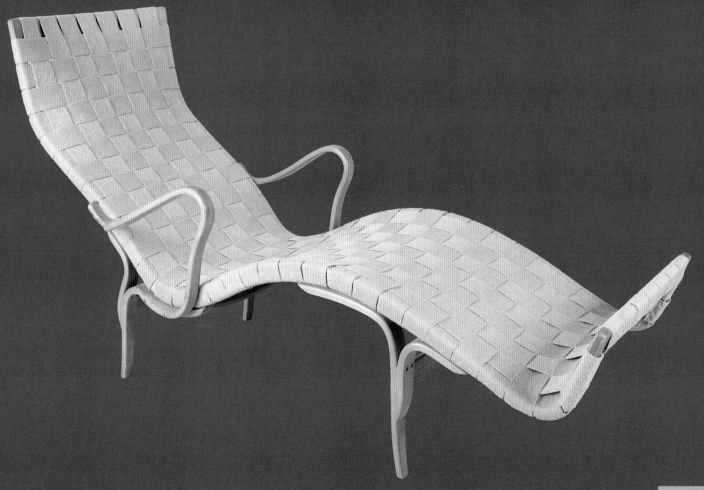

1944

21 Rocking Chair, J16, Hans J. Wegner, FDB Møbler

Hans J. Wegner remarked that he never got a stomach ache when eating cake in his rocking chair. [25] Finding many rockers difficult to get out of and erratic when it came to rocking, the master of organic Modernism controlled his by using less incline on the curve of its feet. With his design the sitter could sit at a reclined angle, rock lightly and lean gently forward to easily get out of the chair without it going completely out of control when you stood up.

"I have always wanted to make unexceptional things of an exceptionally high quality." [26]

Hans J. Wegner

Hans J. Wegner was born in rural Denmark to a cobbler whom he said could "make shoes with his eyes closed". As a regular fixture in his father's workshop, he would play with raw materials he gleaned from building sites where old houses had been torn down, making sculptures as a teenager. At the age of fourteen, Wegner fine-tuned his passion for furniture working for four years as an apprentice to a master cabinetmaker who lived on the same street as his father's shop and workshop.

Wegner studied everything from the work of the American Shaker community to British furniture of the eighteenth and nineteenth centuries at the Technology Institute in Copenhagen and was expecting to set up his own workshop straight after. However the city's famous School of Arts and Crafts spotted his potential

before the end of the course, and he left to learn the Kaare Klint way of measuring older designs in order to be able to reintroduce them in a more modern version. Wegner was spotted at the Copenhagen Cabinetmakers' Guild Exhibition in 1938 while still a student, and was asked to join Arne Jacobsen and Erik Møller creating furniture designs for Aarhus City Hall.

The Wegner Rocking Chair as we know it took form when designer Børge Mogensen saw one Wegner had designed for manufacturer Johannes Hansen and asked him to refine it for FDB, the furniture chain. With his friend's advice, Wegner took out the finger-pinched spindle tops and sinuous wavy armrests to create this rocker that would become a staple in Danish homes. Loved for its comfort, simplicity and elegance, it is still one of the most popular of the larger Wegner chairs and in 1974 was reported by a Danish newspaper to be a firm fixture in both the Vatican and the White House. [27] Created for a variety of shapes, it is much more roomy than the nineteenth-century American Shaker rocker that inspired the J16. To match the rocking chair, Wegner also designed a footstool and leather head support. You sometimes see a fabric seat and back cushion on the chairs in Scandinavian auctions but Wegner's daughter Marianne reports that these were not designed by her father.

Fredericia Furniture now sells the rocking chair in beech and oak in untreated, soap-treated or clear-lacquered versions, as well as in black lacquer. The most iconic of all the designs is the soaped oak version which, for added resale value, is best bought with the matching paper-cord footstool and leather headrest.

1944

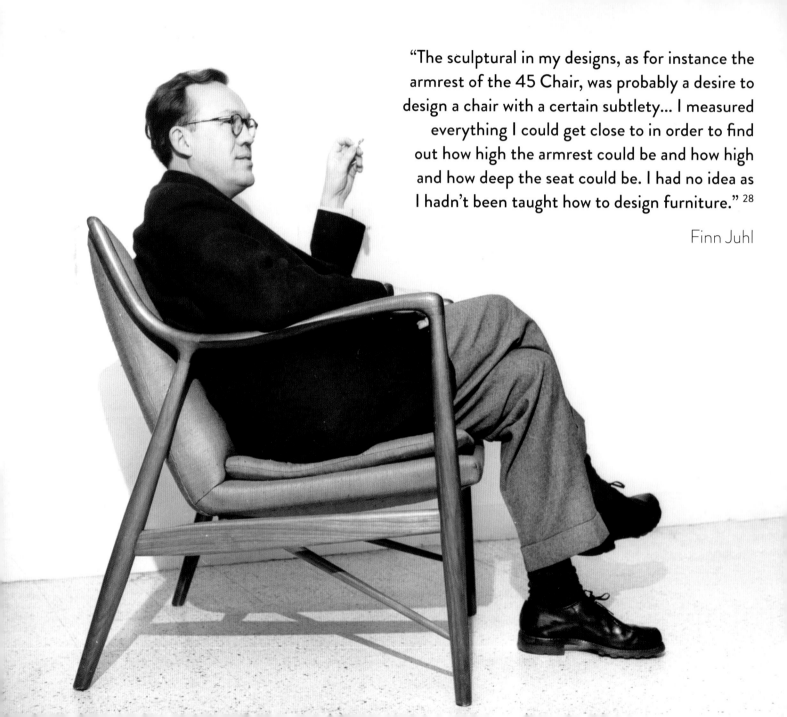

"The sculptural in my designs, as for instance the armrest of the 45 Chair, was probably a desire to design a chair with a certain subtlety... I measured everything I could get close to in order to find out how high the armrest could be and how high and how deep the seat could be. I had no idea as I hadn't been taught how to design furniture." [28]

Finn Juhl

45 Chair, NV45, Finn Juhl, Niels Vodder

Although he appreciated the Functionalist school and believed in comfort and beauty, Finn Juhl's refusal to comply with Kaare Klint's standardized measurements (page 16) made him the subject of criticism. His contemporary Børge Mogensen once accused him of "Mixing cocktail furniture instead of creating applied art for ordinary people." [29] But surely there was room for both in the world of design?

Had he adhered to Klint and Mogensen's strict guidelines for Danish furniture, the 45 Chair with its mix of sharp angles and flowing form would never have existed. Designed in four hours, it walked a tightrope between what had been proved technically possible and his and Vodder's own experimentation with aesthetics, balance and wood engineering. A careful symphony of supporting rods, unconventional joinery and sculpted arms, Juhl's design liberated the seat and back of the lounge chair from the frame, an idea he and Vodder had been working on since he first exhibited his Grasshopper Chair in 1938.

Leading the way for the Chieftain Chair (page 74), the 45 Chair appeared in Cuban mahogany at the 1945 Cabinetmakers' Guild Exhibition in Copenhagen, with a grey curving integrated seat and back and a blue-green seat cushion. Less cumbersome than earlier designs, the modernity and simplicity of the 45 Chair had critics very much warming to the Dane, and is seen as the turning point in his career.

1945

23 DCW (Dining Chair Wood) and LCW (Lounge Chair Wood), Charles and Ray Eames, Evans Products Company

Dubbed "the design of the century" in *Time*'s millennium issue, [30] this plywood chair created in five parts took Charles and Ray on a journey with triumphs and failures along the way. A lesson in moulding plywood into complex curves, it was available in two heights, LCW (page 54) for lounging, DCW (pictured opposite) for dining, with a seat made comfortable by its rubber shock mounts and subtle petal-like edges. Launched at MOMA in 1946 as part of the show "New Furniture Designed by Charles Eames", the exhibition featured a tumbling drum that flipped a range of plywood chairs around to show their durability and was dubbed "a compound of aesthetic brilliance and technical inventiveness" by MOMA's director of industrial design, Eliot Noyes. [31]

It all started when Charles made a press out of a curving plaster mould, scrap wood, heating coils and a bicycle pump and he and Ray started experimenting in their Neutra-designed apartment. Nicknamed the "Kazam", it moulded plywood into curves as if by magic, using wood and glue foraged from the MGM sets Charles worked on at the time. Charles risking life and limb to climb up a pole outside to poach electricity for the machine so they could push the steam-bending experiments of Michael Thonet and Alvar Aalto a step further paid off. Early work with the Kazam led to a huge commission for plywood splints from the Navy during the Second World War. After approaching Evans Products Company in 1943 a new division was created, "Evans Molded Plywood Products", with Charles at the helm and Ray by his side. The splints gave the Eameses the resources to hire staff to go into serious production – eventually they made 150,000 splints, as well as stretchers and glider shells. Money made during the war meant that they could go back to their original plan to mass produce high-quality, affordable chairs when it finished,

something they shared in charming, design-infused courtship letters. As initial prototypes cracked and they had to opt for separate seats and backs, their dream to create a single-shelled chair was forced in another direction, although this in itself proved a triumph as dynamic-looking forms in a variety of woods, with options for fabric, vinyl, leather or hide coverings, appeared out of the constraints. Having never intended to go into retail, Evans found it impossible to juggle both marketing and distribution. So George Nelson, the savvy new design director at Herman Miller, took over the marketing in a cooperation agreement with Evans and the Eameses and by 1949 had also acquired production rights for Herman Miller after Charles was hired as a design consultant.

Because they have evolved over the years with Eames, Herman Miller and Vitra remaining honest to available material and technology, it makes it easier to pin these chairs down to time frames. The screw configuration is the most obvious change. Dealers and collectors have been known to risk buying them with extra screws, hoping to happen upon early prototypes or the first production batch. If you see five screws attaching the front legs, two securing the seat and another five attaching the rear legs (5-2-5), you may have found an LCW or DCW produced at Evans, 1946–1948. Even better if it has some opaquing to the patina and the date stamped on it in black. Herman Miller produced the chair for about a year before Charles and Ray changed the configuration to 5-2-4. Look for early Herman Miller International chairs too (which became Vitra). The Eameses interacted directly with Willi and Rolf Fehlbaum, and the relationship continues between new generations of Eameses and Nora Fehlbaum, CEO of Vitra today.

1945

"We have two types of plywood chairs. One has a metal base and the other has a wood base. Actually I have enjoyed the ones with the metal base the most, because I felt that in a way it divided the function of these two elements. And what I would like to feel is that you walk in the room and not feel conscious of it, I would like to feel conscious of the seat and the back, just as the two would determine the need and that the metal thing would sort of disappear in the room." [32]

Charles Eames

24 Child's Chair, Charles and Ray Eames, Evans Products Company

In 1943 Charles and Ray Eames converted a bus garage at 901 Washington Boulevard, Venice, California into a design workshop, which, within 10 years, would be the kind of casual but industrious studio you would expect from our most inventive companies today. Staff were called on to do everything from contributing to different parts of each piece of furniture to playing or making films. When the circus came to town, everyone was told to pick up a camera and head over to capture their own take on Barnum's circus mastery. Out of this multifaceted work ethic came pieces that were as much for adults as for children including the House of Cards game, Hang-It-All coat rack, wooden spinning tops, a children's furniture line including a sit-on elephant, as well as frogs, seals, horses, bears and tables, and the Eameses' first collaborative foray into mass-produced furniture, the Child's Chair.

Life magazine liked the dinky chair enough to shoot it with other inexpensive goods and useful objects from "An Exhibition for Modern Living" curated in 1949 by Alexander Girard, who was a Michigan based architect at the time. The show, with its room installations created by the Eameses and other behemoths of design including Alvar Aalto and George Nelson, garnered huge amounts of press, but the Child's Chair was never able to reach its full sales potential due to failures in the distribution system.

Earlier, in 1940, Charles Eames and Eero Saarinen had encountered problems with bent ply splitting on their Organic Chair. The Eameses discovered that a chair with a narrower back opening upwards and outwards into another shape eased the pressure on the ply and could take more strain – a lesson Arne Jacobsen later drew on for the Ant (page 100). Because the curving of plywood was much simpler on a chair the size of the Child's Chair it became the first piece to go into mass production, with its matching stool, after the Eameses put plywood splints and plane bodies into production for the war effort.

Created from two lengths of manipulated birch plywood attached with three screws through the seat, the seat and legs are made from one continuous piece with a hammerhead back attached. Ray worked on colour with all kinds of aniline stains including red, blue, yellow, black and magenta and Charles and Ray's love of Swedish folk art was reflected in the heart shape cut-out that doubles as an ingenious handle for two tiny fingers, enabling a child to move the chair from playroom to bathroom before stepping up to reach the sink.

The chair secured a patent but, with Evans not really part of the retail world and Herman Miller seeing no evidence of a market in children's furniture, sales of the chair lagged way below initial expectations. Once the trial run of 5,000 had sold out, no further production followed – until recent years. Vitra's numbered limited production edition (of 2000), produced with Eames Office in 2009, are becoming highly collectable. Surviving chairs from the initial batch of 5,000 now fetch thousands at auction. Keep your eyes peeled. For a much-loved turning-point design the early Child's Chair is still reasonably priced for such a rare collectable and worth snapping up on sight.

1945

25 Womb Chair, 70, Eero Saarinen, Knoll Associates

Early on in their professional relationship, Florence Schust, Hans Knoll's right-hand woman, asked her friend Eero Saarinen to come up with a new type of lounge chair that was different from the long and narrow chairs she was used to; a basket full of pillows she could curl up and read a book in; one she could sit in frontways or sideways. The two had a brother-sister relationship that harked back to the days when "Shu", as she was known, became like an adopted daughter to Eero's father Eliel after he heard that an orphan girl at the local girls' school wanted to study architecture. He asked her to join Cranbrook Academy of Art, the burgeoning arts powerhouse he created that counted Charles and Ray Eames and Harry Bertoia amongst its illustrious students.

> **"The womb chair attempts to achieve a psychological comfort by providing a great big cup-like shell into which you can curl up and pull up your legs, something women especially like to do."** [33]
>
> Eero Saarinen

In 1946, the same year Schust became Mrs Hans Knoll and the company's name was changed to Knoll Associates, Saarinen started experimenting with a paper-cone shape. Folding two sides in to create the arms and seat, he cut off the pointy end, covered the hole, imagined upholstery and a pillow, and something close to the Womb Chair came into being. One of several successful designs in his 70 series, the sculptural piece arose out of his desire to create a chair with no compound curves, one as comfortable for its shape as its cushioning. Moulded using the same process that the Eameses used for their RAR resin shells (page 68) (a process used for wartime shock helmets and boats) and then given latex rubber padding and a fabric cover, the extra cushion added even more womb-like comfort. And while Saarinen struggled with the junction of the plastic with its base (a recurring problem at the time for most chair designers), Saarinen gave the piece elegant metal-rod legs with a chrome or painted finish.

Being reasonably lightweight and devoid of the labour-intensive layers of stuffing employed in earlier lounge chairs, the Womb Chair came at a lower cost to manufacturer and consumer. It took two years of research and prototyping and was manufactured in 1948. Just pipping the Eameses' RAR to become the first mass-produced chair to use a fibre-reinforced, polyester-resin shell. It felt like a breath of fresh air in the American post-war interior, and launched a new era in furniture design.

Now produced in three sizes with matching ottomans, Saarinen's words still ring true: "There seemed to be a need for a large and really comfortable chair to take the place of the old overstuffed chair... Today, more than ever before, we need to relax." [34]

1946

AX Chair, 6020, Peter Hvidt and Orla Mølgaard-Nielsen, Fritz Hansen

In 1947, the year Dior's New Look caused a sensation in Paris and the Cold War began its big freeze between East and West, Peter Hvidt and Orla Mølgaard-Nielsen, an architect and furniture designer respectively, both men, designed a beautiful plywood chair that could easily be dismantled for export without compromising on its Danish good looks. The first Danish chair to boast a seat and back made of double-curved laminate wood, the AX was produced with and without armrests and with reversible leather or canvas upholstery. Testament to its great design, Jack Pritchard, founder of innovative British furniture manufacturer Isokon, had a version – with thin padded upholstery fitted into channels in the wooden frame – in the holiday house he built in Blythburgh, Suffolk, in 1962. This mat (pictured, left) could be removed by pulling it forward from the front of the seat and unscrewing some stretchers.

The AX borrowed a laminating technique from a Danish manufacturer of tennis rackets. Flanked by downswept arms with an Aalto feel, the chair's organic appeal is enlivened by beech ply and mahogany or teak tapering legs that really make the chair stand out from the side. The back and seat slot into a single laminated wood unit of front and back legs with armrests and lock into place with spindles between the legs. This construction meant it could be made quickly, without compromising on standards, and take up less space and packaging for transport than manufacturing had previously seen. Accompanied by the AX Table and exhibited in 1951 as part of the Good Design show sponsored by MOMA, Hvidt and Mølgaard's knock-down chair became a huge success for Fritz Hansen who produced it throughout the fifties until the seventies.

LEFT: The AX Chair could be knocked down easily for export, as seen here.

1947

ABOVE: In their pursuit for perfection, Hans J. Wegner and Johannes Hansen were rigorous in their attention to detail.

While the starker styles of Modernism were being touted across Europe, Hans J. Wegner, in collaboration with master cabinetmaker Johannes Hansen, stuck to his roots as a skilled cabinetmaker. Rather than ignore the lessons taught by centuries of furniture making in Denmark, he worked with the tools of his trade to push chair making to its limit. The Windsor chair had been on his mind since he and other students took measurements of a nineteenth-century comb-back Windsor as part of the course at the Copenhagen School of Arts and Crafts. This English prototype had morphed and developed a style of its own in America and Europe. But here "Wegner's Windsor", as it was originally called by the media, is transformed into a proud "Peacock", the name given to it by fellow designer Finn Juhl, with spindles flattened into a rainbow where the sitter's back needs most support, and a proud sweep of a hooped back exaggerated to give it a throne-like

quality. What was previously seen as a modest domestic chair with an arc laminated out of several pieces "Is now made from a single piece of wood using the pre-compression technique where you put an already steamed piece of wood under pressure from the ends while keeping it straight. It is rounded in a special machine to be thicker at the ends and thinner in the middle. Finally it is bent and dried while keeping the shape fixed," according to Wegner's daughter Marianne. Like the Shakers, Wegner chose to weave his seat. The paper cord softens the harder structure of the ash frame below. The teak armrests matched a table in the same collection but were "primarily to hide the grease and dirt from users' hands" [35] according to Marianne. Besides ash with either teak or ash armrests, PP Møbler, producer since 1992, now also include the chair in oak, with oak or teak armrests.

"In a good Windsor, lightness, strength, grace, durability and quaintness are all found in an irresistible blend," American furniture historian Wallace Nutting wrote in *A Windsor Handbook* in 1917. Wegner's Windsor had it all and more, with every angle calculated and recalculated and the design refined – from the curve of the back to the wedge detailing he added to the top of the front legs to fasten them to the seat. Designer Hella Jongerius is a big fan of Wegner's Peacock Chair. When she refurnished the North Delegates' Lounge at the United Nations' New York headquarters in 2013, the only furniture from the sixties not given the chop was a row of proud Peacocks. See over (page 64) for how to look after the paper cord seat on a Peacock Chair and Wishbone Chair.

"The goal is to express something in wood
that is natural for the wood – to discover
what is right, carpentry-wise. Look at
the Windsor chair, a simple construction,
something the people of England were
able to make 200 years ago. But it is also
a distinctive design, precisely because it
expresses what it is so naturally." [36]

Hans J. Wegner

1947

How to look after paper cord

The woven paper cord seats seen in many of Hans J. Wegner's chairs require little maintenance as the strong paper cord is designed to last for years and patinate over time. If you do want to freshen up the seat, perhaps once or twice a year, follow these instructions.

Wipe the paper cord seat with a soft cloth and soap solution (made from 1½ tbsp undyed soap flakes mixed with 5 litres/10 pints lukewarm water). It is advisable not to do this too often as it can wear or fluff up the paper cord.

Seats made of natural paper cord can be discoloured by dyed fabrics, like the indigo dye on a pair of new jeans. To prevent this from happening, use a cushion on the seat.

The best paper cord will be treated with a thin layer of wax to prevent stains, but it will not be able to combat grease, red wine, fruit juice or the strong colour of spices in curry powder. To treat stains, remove as much of the fluid as possible with a soft cloth wrung out with lukewarm water and blot the affected area. Do not rub.

Never use washing-up liquid on paper cord or soaped oak.

If you need a visual guide, Carl Hansen & Søn have produced a video to show you how to look after paper cord and soaped oak.

RIGHT: Master craftsman Benny Hammer Larsen, Carl Hansen & Søn's top weaver, working on the paper cord seat of a Wishbone Chair.

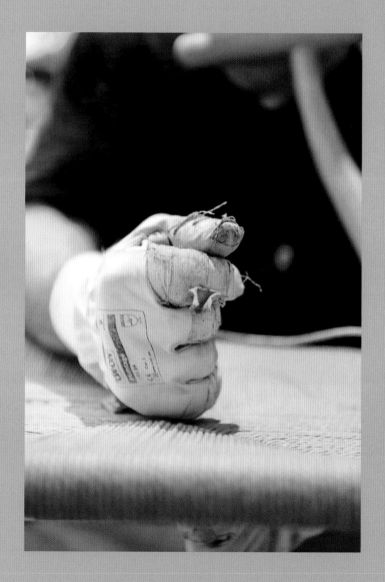

Model 132U, Don Knorr, Knoll and Associates

It is doubtful that Don Knorr would have entered MOMA's 1948 International Competition for Low-Cost Furniture Design and won first prize for seating were it not for Eero Saarinen. Knorr had been helping draw up plans for Saarinen's upholstered 70 series, which included the Womb Chair (page 58), by day while thrashing out new ideas with his mentor at night for two years preceding the competition. When Knorr first showed Saarinen the idea for his chair in 1947, the famous architect and designer told his protégé to go back to basics. Without this input, Knorr's entry would have looked a lot more complicated.

The 1948 prototype of the winning chair can be seen at MOMA, with its thick thermal plastic shell set on chromed tubular steel legs. Hans Knoll wanted to produce the chair, but production costs proved too high, so Knoll had Knorr work with his engineers to turn the award-winning idea into a piece in sheet steel that would be comfortable, sculptural and include shapes and fixtures created to make manufacture and storage a doddle. "The first thing I learned from Hans Knoll was that the major cost of getting a product started was the casts and moulds," said Knorr. "My design eliminated all that." [37]

As Knoll sent the 1949 version of his design to the production line in 1950, Knorr headed into the San Francisco sunset to work for architects Skidmore, Owings and Merrill. He established his own practice, Don Knorr and Associates, in 1951 and was one of twenty-three practices to take part in the bold Case Study House Program that reimagined modern living using new industrial materials and techniques developed during and after the war. Knorr's contribution was the 1969 Scoren house which he worked on with textile designer

and sculptor Alexander Girard who came up with the idea for a three-metre (ten-foot) tall double entrance door that jumbled up mirror image letters from the owner's name to create a playful game. Led by *Arts & Architecture* magazine's then-editor John Entenza, the programme envisioned affordable single-family homes in California built in a Modernist style at affordable prices. But nothing Knorr did quite eclipsed his flexible and elegant chair. Produced with or without upholstery (with the same latex rubber filling as Saarinen's Womb Chair) it looks light and yet sculptural enough to be a stand-alone piece in a room.

29 Listen-To-Me Chaise, 4873, Edward J Wormley, Dunbar

While the design world at large was looking towards industrial production and canny manufacturing techniques, the Indiana-based fine furnishing company Dunbar stayed faithful to handmaking each piece in the finest materials with the help of a bright young spark named Edward J Wormley.

Dunbar was lucky to snap up this talented designer, who returned to America brimming with ideas, following a trip to Paris, where he met architect Le Corbusier and the Art Deco furniture designer Émile-Jacques Ruhlmann. Wormley not only proved to be a whizz at creating sophisticated designs with immaculate craftsmanship, his laser-sharp observation made him an expert at marketing too.

When Wormley returned to Dunbar after the war he spotted that a percentage of customers picked whole suites from the collections rather than ordering one or two pieces in the shops, but the sales team would report back that the suites had gaps in them – customers were asking for other pieces for their rooms. Wormley spotted a sales opportunity and Dunbar saw their profits soar after the designer plugged the gaps with designs of his own.

Wormley's traditional-meets-contemporary style, which he saw as transitional, proved so popular that he was given free rein to create a collection of his own each year, on the understanding that he would also produce a traditional Dunbar collection. But it soon became clear that the more contemporary pieces were more popular than the old-fashioned lines and Dunbar switched exclusively to Wormley's modern collections from 1944. By 1945 Wormley's confidence had grown. While he stayed in touch as a consultant, giving him access to the Dunbar marketing machine, he left the company to set up a New York studio in his own name and soak up the Manhattan design scene. Free to dream up ideas like his iconic wooden Magazine Tree and the A-Frame Chair he sits in for that famous July 1961 *Playboy* shoot, his ideas just got better and better.

> ## "Modernism means freedom – freedom to mix, to choose, to change, to embrace the new but to hold fast to what is good." [38]
>
> ## Edward J Wormley

Now an icon of American Modernism, Wormley's Listen-To-Me Chaise, constructed from laminated white maple and American cherry, was the perfect "thinking" chair for the *Mad Men*-type executive strung out on booze and stress. But with its quilted woollen fabric sewn with a metal thread to echo the copper wire support below, women loved it too. Sophisticated, sexy, country-club style like you had never seen it before, it featured on the balcony of writer Barbara Novak's New York apartment in the film *Down With Love* and is "the Holy Grail for Dunbar collectors" [39] according to New York dealer Patrick Parrish. It is still seen as one of Wormley's most elegant designs.

1948

30 RAR (Rocking Armchair Rod), Charles and Ray Eames, Herman Miller

Films the Eameses created may have given people the sense that life in "the shop", as Ray called it, was an endless play session but the best chairs would often take years to develop. Once a really good chair had taken form in their hands and been tested by countless shapes and sizes it would often start a chain reaction that gave birth to a much larger collection.

Initially modelled in neoprene-coated aluminium, the RAR evolved from a stamped metal chair the Eameses worked on with engineers at UCLA after they were partnered up for MOMA's Low Cost Furniture Design competition. Charles and Ray first encountered a form of fibreglass while designing sliding screens for the Eames House. Originally used for shock helmets during the war, the durable mix of glass fibres and plastic resin seemed the perfect antidote to high-cost metal so the problem-solving partners called in reps from plastic manufacturers Zenith who, following a rather convoluted discussion which involved Charles giving them a lesson in colour, determined to reconvene.

To further understand the material, Charles took a craft paper model to Californian boatbuilder John Wills. When he saw how it could be made out of a process Wills had developed of curing fibreglass at room temperature, he ordered a prototype to prove the idea to himself – and to Herman Miller. Then they found Zenith who even shared costs with Herman Miller and were able to assist the Eameses in developing the world's first mass-produced plastic shell chair. Initial costs were high. The "Zenaloy" sheets had to be pressed in hydraulic moulds adapted from shipbuilding technology.

The first two thousand shells produced had an embedded rope edge and car giant Chrysler was called upon to create shock mounts. After two years of development, interchangeable metal and wood leg-systems were introduced and a "low-cost", lightweight rocking chair emerged as part of a family of chairs exploring how furniture could adapt to different needs and environments. The Eameses chose three colours for their neutral quality. While the elephant grey proved quite challenging, greige or creamy parchment were less likely to fade in the process of embedding colour into the fibreglass using pressure. Early on in the production, Ray added the iconic seafoam colour along with yellow and red. Upholstered Hopsack shells designed with Herman Miller's textile director Alexander Girard were introduced in 1952. Chairs at this time with a "Miller-Zenith" label would have been designed between 1950 and 53. The non-upholstered range expanded to sixteen colours by 1963 and even though production ceased in 1968 Herman Miller's commitment to present its pregnant employees with RARs as a company gift continued until the mid-eighties.

The Eames spirit of "Getting the most of the best to the greatest number of people for the least" was very much alive when Vitra reintroduced the range in 1998 with environmentally friendly polypropylene seats based on some of Charles and Ray Eameses' plastic chair designs from the seventies, and many from McDonald's to the Los Angeles County Museum of Art adopted the lower-cost Eames plastic chairs, however a less volatile, monomer-free "dry bind" process was also developed with the fibreglass striation for those who prefer the look of vintage shells.

1948-50

DSW (Dining Side Wood), Charles and Ray Eames, Herman Miller, 1948–50

At their debut at the Low-Cost Furniture Design competition, both the fibreglass strengthened plastic armchair and side chair were offered with different bases. The single-shell chair soon became a feature in schools, restaurants, homes and offices in various incarnations including the DSW (Dining Side Wood) with a wooden dowel leg, and the metal legged DSX (Dining Shell X-base) and DSR (Dining Side Rod) also known as the Eiffel base after Paris' Eiffel Tower.

> **"In architecture, or furniture, or jack straws, it's the connection that can do you in. Where two materials come together, brother, watch out."** [40]
>
> Charles Eames

By 1950, the original rope edging had gone and seats could be stacked or attached to metal rods and put together in rows, to create the Tandem Shell Seating scheme for airports and stadiums. "What works is better than what looks good," said Ray Eames. "The 'looks good' can change, but what works, WORKS." [41]

The plastic family evolved, with changes happening over the years to improve the chair. There was an answer to every problem with the Eameses, who loved working with constraints. The curve of the back became more inclined for comfort and the edges of the seat redrafted to make a smoother line. Ever the pragmatist as well as the dreamer, Charles Eames put rejected fibreglass shells back into production by having them upholstered after he found ones affected by discolouration were being consigned to the office skip.

31 Colonial Chair, OW149, Ole Wanscher, A.J. Iversen

Although he is not as publicly recognized as design greats Arne Jacobsen or Hans J. Wegner, Danish designer Ole Wanscher is the craftsman's craftsman. Classical and modern, functional and elegant, his work sits effortlessly across a timeline of chair design and is equally comfortable beside a Thomas Chippendale or a Finn Juhl chair.

Take his most famous piece: the Colonial Chair he designed in 1949 while working with master joiner A.J. Iversen. Supported

by impossibly thin sections of Danish wood, it is the proportional distribution that has furniture designers in awe. The way the arm sweeps up a little to meet the back post; the meeting of rail between front and back leg; the outward curve of the legs at the back; and the spigot joints that lock sections together. All of this creates a chair of immense strength and durability that still looks beautiful, light to the touch and, when you get your head around the technical achievement, takes your breath away. The human is imagined in the chair at every point in the design process, from the ends of the armrests to the most luxurious leather cushions filled with feathers. Four bars of wood support the back with a leather cushion held in place by small leather loops. Even the hand-woven reed seat can be lifted out and re-caned without sending the whole chair back to the producer.

Author of books including *The History of the Art of Furniture: Five Thousand Years of Furniture*, Wanscher acquired his fascination for furniture while travelling with his art historian father. But it was his love of eighteenth-century English furniture design that came to the fore in his Colonial Chair. He was introduced to the work of Thomas Chippendale and to campaign chairs used by British officers abroad while a student of Kaare Klint at the Royal Academy of Fine Arts in Copenhagen, so it was serendipitous that Ole Wanscher would take Klint's place as Head of the Furniture Department after Klint died in 1954. Produced for the mass market with P. Jeppesen in the mid-fifties, and now part of the Carl Hansen & Søn oeuvre with its matching Colonial Coffee Table (1949) and Colonial Sofa (1964), Wanscher's Colonial Chair would not look out of place anywhere.

1949

Antropus, 721, Marco Zanuso, Ar-flex

Marco Zanuso wanted to give form to what he called complexity. One of the leading exponents of the Modern design movement in Italy and co-editor of both *Domus* and *Casabella* magazines, he is also remembered for a revolutionary child's plastic side chair he designed with Richard Sapper between 1959 and 1964. However it is his signature work with its foam and rubber strapping that paved the way for some of the most elegantly upholstered chairs of the fifties.

Chemist Eric Owen first developed latex foam rubber for seating on public transport and bed mattresses with British firm Dunlop in 1929. But it was not until architect Franco Albini happened upon a polyurethane foam (derived originally from German scientists) and drew designs of chairs using what he called "gommapiuma" as a replacement for rubber latex in a catalogue for his stand at the 1936 Milan Triennale, that Italian rubber tyre manufacturer Pirelli saw a way they could expand into new areas, like Dunlop, but without tapping into their precious rubber resources. The designer part of the puzzle came after the Pirelli team spotted a chair that Zanuso had designed for MOMA's 1948 Low-Cost Furniture Design competition that joined a fabric seat to a metal frame. Pirelli loved it so much that a whole new furniture division called Ar-flex (later Arflex) was set up to hothouse this new Italian superstar. Zanuso and Pirelli's engineers set about creating a new diaphragm for seating using the polyurethane foam and nastrocord (a reinforced elastic strap similar to the rubber sandows René Herbst had used in the late twenties) to replace the cumbersome springs that traditional chairs and car seats were lumbered with at the time.

And so a new style of upholstery began to emerge in Italy just as the post-war depression dust started to clear. Soft and delicate in form, but ample and comfortable, Antropus, with its solid wood outer structure and thin layer of foam and fabric, arose out of the first experiments – with side panels acting as both feet and armrests and an internal steel frame holding nastrocord springs and foam padding in a structured hammock. Invited to dress the set for Thornton Wilder's *The Skin of Our Teeth,* Zanuso launched his armchair on stage in one of the first comedies performed at the Piccolo Teatro in Milan at the end of the forties, and a theatre Zanuso helped redesign in 1998. From the side, Antropus, now produced by Cassina, made the actors look like they were suspended in magnificent sculptures.

33 Chieftain Chair, Finn Juhl, Niels Vodder

After a twenty minute bidding war at the Phillips "Nordic Design" auction in London in September 2013, an early Chieftain Chair designed by Finn Juhl and executed by Niels Vodder became the world record holder for the highest price ever achieved in antique Scandinavian furniture. Estimated at anywhere between £50,000 and £75,000 it reached a staggering £422,500, elevating Finn Juhl's furniture to art collector status.

The Chieftain Chair originally got its name after the King of Denmark tried it for size at an exhibition and a journalist suggested Juhl call it "The King's chair". "I'd prefer The Chieftain's chair," the founding father of Danish Modern design replied, having been inspired by ancient tribal weaponry. Juhl went on to win five gold medals at the Milan Triennale during the fifties.

Few chairs come close to evoking as much emotion in collectors as the Chieftain Chair. How it manages to look almost alive, a creature about to rise from its camouflaged perch and perform its ritual love-making dance on a plant, remains master craftsman Niels Vodder's secret. Certainly the way Juhl designed it, with the leather armrest and seat cut free showing thinly upholstered surfaces floating above a teak frame, gives the chair a stick-insect quality. Proud in its nakedness, with each element flowing seamlessly into another, Juhl's sinuous design was certainly in strong contrast to the Functionalist geometry of the time, led by his college professor Kaare Klint. Juhl did not believe in blindly passing on tradition; he appreciated the grace of Art Nouveau's curves as much as Le Corbusier's architecture and the abstract sculpture of the time. While he did believe in stripping things away, he picked comfort over the lean look of his contemporaries' work. Expressive and organic, Juhl's designs gave just the right amount of support in exacting minimal proportions.

It was a particular brand of joinery that put incredible demands on Vodder, without whom Juhl would never have succeeded. Juhl studied architecture and was untrained as a cabinetmaker. He was not limited in being able to express his artistic idiom, but machines could not produce his biomorphic creations. "He was agitating for industrialism," according to Hans Henrik Sørensen, founding partner of Onecollection, the company chosen by Juhl's late wife as the main producer of his furniture. "But his organic aesthetic was not easily processed. When Finn Juhl tried to adopt his design for industrial production in the 1950s they did not look as spectacular as they did in the 1940s." [42]

Appropriate prices depend on the production run. The seventy original rosewood and leather Chieftain Chairs with Niels Vodder's name on them, originally bought for Danish embassies around the world, now fetch astronomical prices. Sørensen suggests picking Soren Horn over Niels Roth Andersen. "Any cabinetmaker who has made the Chieftain Chair added his personal touch. A Baker-produced model will not command as much as the later Horn or Andersen versions, although our version has four buttons in the back instead of the more popular three because the Chieftain Chair in Finn Juhl's home has four buttons, and we believe it is the first chair from the Cabinetmakers' Guild Exhibition in 1949."

"It's a serious matter", Sørensen quips. "Sometimes a small war can break out between dedicated Juhl nerds over things like this." [43]

1949

"One shouldn't despair over the fact that some of the developments one has hoped for were never produced but only turned out to be a beginning. Perhaps they will be revived some day in the future, if necessary, when the time is ripe."[44]

Finn Juhl

34 Round Chair, JH503, Hans J. Wegner, Johannes Hansen

Americans call it "The Chair"; Hans J. Wegner called it "The Round One". Brits used to call it "The Classic Chair". Originally knocked up in forty-eight hours, the earlier JH501 version was made from oak with a rattan seat with rattan wrapped around the back of the top rail to hide joins where the wood curved around the back. The rattan was removed when Wegner perfected a wedged tenon with a faint zigzag pattern to replace the joins a year later, and a rattan-seated chair with a clean back (and matching upholstered version) was put into production in 1950 as JH503.

Inspired by the Eameses and Alvar Aalto and intrigued by research into the bent plywood used in British aeroplanes, Wegner looked like he was heading in a different direction years before he designed the Round Chair. He even participated in MOMA's Low-Cost Furniture Design competition in 1948 using this new material. But after the Round Chair was leaped upon by Americans hungry for craft in combination with modern design following the war, Wegner realized it would be to the advantage of Johannes Hansen's workshop to stick to what they knew. Prototypes for moulded shells cost money every time you wanted to adjust something. He saw how making changes to solid wood was easier and more efficient. He also felt honour-bound to perfect The Chair and carried on doing so throughout his life with many of his later designs reflecting this.

An elegantly curved design consisting of eleven pieces of wood with arms that wrap around the sitter and join to the legs either side of the back on the top rail, "This precise cut between the arm and back was made in order to give the glue the best conditions for keeping the three pieces of wood together. But just as ingenious is the system joinery between the four rails in the seat frame hidden in the legs", [45] according to Wegner's daughter Marianne. Wegner fine-tuned the proportions until he had a chair that could provide enough comfort between the carved backrest and the seat itself, while allowing the sitter freedom to move. "Your rear end needs room," [46] he said.

A club in Chicago ordered 400 chairs after "The Round One" was photographed and credited in an article in the February 1950 issue of *Interiors* magazine and, even though manufacturer Johannes Hansen was not confident the company could fulfil such an order, the club persisted and two years later 400 Round Chairs arrived in containers and America's love affair with Wegner was consummated. Worldwide fame followed in 1960 when Richard Nixon and John F. Kennedy were presented with "The Chair" to sit on by channel TNC's Danish furniture-loving owner for the first ever televised political debate. It became a silent but confident symbol of change at this historic event, which led to the unseating of the Republican government.

The Round Chair has been copied so many times that master-craftsman manufacturer Johannes Hansen was able to lay his hands on twelve of the copies which he exhibited at his company's fiftieth jubilee in 1965 where he celebrated twenty-five years of collaboration with Hans J. Wegner. Marianne Wegner says her father saw it as less of a joke. He once complained to a journalist that he could hardly come up with a new idea before it was copied by somebody else, which meant that he or his manufacturer barely had their expenses covered.

1949

"Personally I think it [Round Chair] is my best achievement. Not because of its export success, but because I have been more thorough with it than anything else." [47]

Hans J. Wegner

Hans J. Wegner
TOP 10

Hans J. Wegner is widely considered one of the leading figures in twentieth-century furniture design and the driving force in the Danish Modern movement that changed the way people looked at furniture in the fifties and sixties. He designed more than 500 chairs throughout his lifetime and had more than 100 produced. Widely copied, he has influenced so many famous designers.

Here are his top 10 chairs:

Rocking Chair 1944 (page 48)

Peacock Chair 1947 (page 62)

Round Chair 1949 (page 78)

Wishbone Chair 1949 (page 84)

Flag Halyard Chair 1950

Papa Bear Chair 1950-1 (page 88)

Valet Chair 1953 (page 116)

Swivel Chair 1955

The Ox Chair 1960

Three Legged Shell Chair 1963

Folding Chair, JH512, Hans J. Wegner, Johannes Hansen

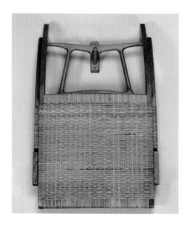

When Danish designer Hans J. Wegner and master cabinetmaker Johannes Hansen first produced chairs for the Cabinetmakers' Guild Exhibitions in Copenhagen, Wegner felt, "It was more like a game. We had to have something novel to display every Autumn. I drew it and Johannes Hansen made it. We were happy if we could sell the chairs we had made for the exhibition. This was as far as our hopes went." [48] But their mission to make wood come alive struck a chord with visitors, and since 1949 there was never a show where they did not have to meet extra orders.

The Folding Chair in solid wood and cane pays reference to Mies van der Rohe's Barcelona Chair in the lean of its back and seat. But, unlike the Barcelona Chair, which was based on a Roman magistrate's stool and was never intended to fold, Wegner curved his feet in two directions to allow for the flattest finish when folding. Wooden handles enable the sitter to push themselves up from a low position, and also add strength to the construction while offering up a lovely side silhouette. "I think that my father is unique in his way of showing rather than hiding difficult design issues," says Marianne Wegner. "In fact he often draws your attention to them through his choice of solution,

like where he adds the handle and crosses the cane in the gap of the weaving." [49] Wegner was often inspired by the tools in his workshop and the front handle at each side of the chair is reminiscent of the handle of a saw.

"He had a very down to earth attitude towards his furniture, namely that they were useful tools. A chair was not a good or pretty chair if you did not sit well in it." [50]

Marianne Wegner

The Folding Chair comes with a hook designed for mounting the chair closed, with its legs upright on the wall. Presented with his soon-to-be world famous Round Chair (page 78) at a Cabinetmakers' Guild Exhibition in 1949 it was the perfect answer for people with small apartments and, while it was shamelessly plagiarized, many copyists failed to notice, or decided to ignore, the two small waves in the stretcher between the legs which ensure the chair doesn't slide to one or the other side when hanging. While her father was frustrated by shoddy attempts to reproduce his work, "Leaving out the waves at least made it possible to distinguish between the original and the copies," says Marianne, who adds, "How much this little detail meant was not so obvious to everybody, since I know of one museum in Germany and one in Britain which bought a copy for their collection thinking it was the original. This was not revealed until years later." [51]

1949

36 Wishbone Chair, CH24, Hans J. Wegner, Carl Hansen & Søn

No book on chairs could be published without some mention of the most popular Wegner chair, the Wishbone, or Y Chair, which takes its name from the slim flattened rib in its back that arches out to meet a top rail that nestles under your arms. Holger Hansen (son of Carl Hansen) asked Wegner to produce something similar to the China Chair he designed for Fritz Hansen (no relation) in 1943, but Wegner was keen to try his hand at a lighter and more modern version that could be put into mass production. By using a "Y" as support for the steam bent back and armrest and by giving the back legs a twist forward from the seat in order to bring them up to support the arms, he was able to give this new dining chair a more sculptural form than earlier incarnations. Furthermore, the lower, shorter arms allowed the chair to come closer to the table while giving the sitter a huge amount of movement.

The producers and designer agreed on paper cord for the seat so that everything could be made in-house, according to Wegner's daughter, Marianne. "What Carl Hansen & Søn needed was something to keep the production running in order to survive, since times were bad shortly after World War Two. Earlier, seaweed would have been chosen, but this couldn't be bought in the right length and quality suited for the job. So instead they tried paper cord, which time has shown was stronger and not as elastic as seaweed." [52] The seat is intricately hand-woven by a team taught by dedicated master craftsmen. Benny Hammer Larsen, who has worked for the company for more than two decades, has a Wishbone tattoo gracing the inside of one arm in reverence to his favourite chair. The 120 metres (394 feet) of paper cord he weaves in the space of one hour can last up to fifty years, thanks to the tight packing of the cord and some carefully formed knots underneath. Many have tried to fix the paper cord on Wegner seats but some come unstuck when it comes to the knots as they are often seen as a mistake. The weaver would not be able to weave the chair in one long piece, so they use several pieces, allowing a tighter weave that lasts a longer time.

Often referred to as the supermodel of chairs for the amount of front cover splashes it gets on interiors magazines around the world, the Wishbone Chair has been in continual production since 1950. The genius of it, as with many of Wegner's chairs, is that it manages to look strikingly minimal, despite the 100 production steps, many of which are done by hand. It is now produced in two heights – the original version in the original height still suits the Asian market but Europeans and Americans have grown larger over the years and Carl Hansen & Søn have therefore been allowed to make this version 2cm (¾ in) higher.

1949

How to look after a classic soaped-oak Wegner chair

1. Apply a soap solution (made from 1½ tbsp soap flakes mixed with 5 litres/10 pints of lukewarm water) using a dry cloth or sponge and sweep in the direction of the grain.

2. Wait about ten minutes.

3. Tightly wring out the cloth with hot water and wipe the chair to remove excess soap.

4. Allow the chair to dry.

5. If the wood fibres rise slightly after the first few soap treatments, you might sand gently, using 240-grit sandpaper. Always sand in the direction of the grain.

6. For everyday care, use a clean, soft cloth wrung out with lukewarm water. Do not use wire wool, washing-up liquid, oils or any cleaning agents or chemicals on the chair.

See page 64 for how to look after paper cord.

Side Chair, 939, Ray Komai, J.G. Furniture Systems

Greatly influenced by the abstract artists of the day including Paul Klee and Pablo Picasso, Los Angeles born Ray Komai took new developments in ply from the Eameses and gave them an African twist. Fascinated by tribal masks from Africa and New Guinea, his 939 Side Chair bears a cheeky resemblance to a human face.

The folded ply Side Chair was designed four years after Komai was relocated from the Manzanar Japanese internment camp, where he worked as a designer in the industrial division and enjoyed folding paper and small chips of ply into shapes, imagining chairs he would design on his release. One of many Japanese designers born and raised in America and imprisoned during the Second World War, he settled in Washington DC, but soon moved to New York with his wife where he got a job as a layout artist and then textile designer for Laverne Originals, New York's top interior company of the time, before eventually opening his own design studio.

The earliest model of the Side Chair with its wooden legs was made in Brooklyn by a division of Pennsylvanian company J.G. Furniture Systems and received a Good Design Award by MOMA in 1950. Seen here, it was also produced with chromed metal legs in order to make it stackable – a version which the designer's daughter Tami Komai owned. She saw the chair with wooden legs for the first time in a German design magazine in 2014, having always had the practical version with bent tubular-steel legs at home.

1949

38 Papa Bear Chair, AP19, Hans J. Wegner, A.P. Stolen

The AP19 got its pet name after a journalist at the time said it looked like a giant teddy bear coming to wrap its arms around you. Ardent fans of Wegner may have spotted it in the living room in Samantha and Darrin's house in the sixties TV series *Bewitched*.

Originally fashioned out of plasticine in 1950, as Wegner did with all his upholstered chairs, Papa Bear employs a superbly crafted beech frame that was created from the outset by PP Møbler. The original suppliers of the skeleton now produce the chair in all its glory, but it was A.P. Stolen that first added the cotton, palm, tow, coil springs and horse hair to the chair. Different materials with different properties are essential to ensuring the Papa Bear's shape and comfort, much like a properly tailored suit. Coil springs are sewn into bags of linen fabric and then on to jute straps. The internal sides of the chair are padded with shaped tow and then covered with horsehair and cotton before being upholstered

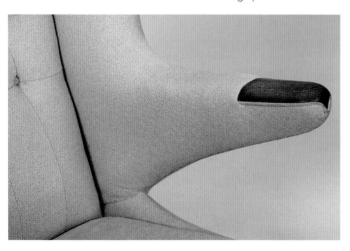

and tightened by the addition of buttons which give the chair its ergonomic shape. Unlike most other comfortable easy chairs, the only foam is in the seat's cushion. Originally upholstered in wool, the bulk was stripped right back to make it the most lightweight of armchairs, although the cantilevered structure meant it was as sturdy as its traditional counterparts.

Armrests were cut free from the seat for lightness and ease of movement. "Paws" in oak, teak, cherry or rosewood made it just that little bit more hard-wearing and exclusive. The arms were designed with a gap underneath for practical reasons. Here was an armchair you could move your legs around in: stick them through the side and not just over the arms but also under the arms; or one leg over, one leg under. Wegner understood people could be restless and he loved to move around when reading or listening to music: "I like a chair to be so large that you can really see it and burrow yourself into it," [53] he said, giving the back of the chair cushioned edges you could nestle your face into.

When the chair was kickstarted Wegner production at PP Møbler in 2003, reintroduced as the PP19, they had to cut up mattresses to get the coil springs they needed, according to Matthew Rhodes at the Cale Schiang Partnership, specialists in Modern Scandinavian furniture. Now upholstered in fabric or leather, with an eye-wateringly high starting price, the Papa Bear is the Rolls Royce of designer chairs, costing several times a Mies van der Rohe Barcelona Chair. For real authenticity, the most ardent fans buy it with the matching footstool.

1950-1

Hillestak, Robin Day, S. Hille and Co., 1951 (U leg model), mid-1950s (V leg model)

In 1947 Rosamind, the daughter of Ray Hille, owner and driving force behind S. Hille and Co., and Rosamind's husband Leslie Julius went on a trip that would change the direction of their reproduction furniture company forever. The Hille directors stopped by the Herman Miller showroom and, after pawing over the bent-ply creations of a young upstart called Charles Eames who was causing a stir in the design world, they made it their mission to find their own Eames closer to home.

They snapped up Robin Day after he won an award for a storage system with Clive Latimer at MOMA's 1948 International Competition for Low-Cost Furniture Design. Within a week of their first meeting he produced the famous lower-case Hille logo. As well as furniture, he took on all the graphics and showroom designs gratis for the first ten years in return for free rein to design whatever he wanted with access to the technology required.

Day put new plastic glues through their paces to produce a lightweight stacking chair with a walnut or teak-covered ply back and seat, linked with a laminated spine on a beech frame. While he was only able to bend wood one way at this stage, it remained in production for four years after his Polyprop Chair went into production in 1963, thanks to huge orders from schools, canteens and church halls. Liberty took the design on and sold them to ply-lovers for 66 shillings each and international licensees made Hille a name around the world. Forever improving on designs, Day's daughter Paula remembers how he regularly brought samples back from the Hille factory in Watford. "He once told me a story about an important client, who inadvertently sat on a prototype in the hall, not realizing the seat wasn't fixed to the base." [54]

Collectors often buy the Hillestak chair with the matching Hillestak table or desk with its drawer unit suspended underneath. Day also designed a set of office accessories – filing tray, blotter, wooden calendar and wastepaper bin – which is highly sought after by midcentury collectors.

1951

40 Antelope Chair, Ernest Race, Race Furniture

Jack Pritchard, the founder of Isokon, who met Race when he was a draughtsman for lighting firm Troughton & Young, once said that the Antelope Chair, the most renowned of Ernest Race's designs, had "wit and elegance". A grand departure from anything that had gone before, like good china used for tea, there was certainly something refined and British about it. Pritchard and his Bauhaus friends, Walter Gropius and Marcel Breuer, were regular visitors to a shop that Race opened in London in 1937 where hand-woven textiles in a Bauhaus-inspired design were sold alongside furniture designed by Gerald Summers. The combination was a hit with the hippest architects and designers of the day.

When war was declared in September 1939, plywood was diverted to the aircraft industry and manufacturers were banned from producing anything other than utility furniture for victims of bombings. When the embargo was lifted in 1948, designers started scrabbling around for whatever wood was left over. Inventive entrepreneurs including British engineer J.W. Noel Jordan looked elsewhere. After discovering some redundant tooling that had been used to bend aluminium and steel rods during the war, Jordan posted an advertisement in *The Times* to find an upcoming designer to help him mass produce furniture in metal. Ernest Race applied and the skilled draughtsman and lighting designer immediately hit it off. Race only had a few bits of unit furniture to his name but he recognized that Jordan had the engineering skill to turn his drawings into something workable. Engineer and designer worked seamlessly together, with Jordan happy for Race to take all the glory; and it was with a sense of adventure that Race Furniture was born.

In 1946 the dynamic duo showcased a repurposed chair made from recast aluminium – sourced from redundant British warplanes – with a plate aluminium seat upholstered in parachute silk at the "Britain Can Make It" exhibition at the Victoria & Albert Museum. Fifteen hundred BA3 chairs and tables were purchased by the government for troop ships. Heal & Son and Dunn's snapped them up, eager to satisfy the design-hungry post-war public. It was upcycling with guts, and people loved it. Success with the BA3 led to Race winning a commission from the 1951 Festival of Britain to manufacture furniture for cafes and terraces across the whole South Bank site. The Springbok, a chair stripped back to the bare tension springs, and the Antelope, an intricate skeleton with white frame and a fun floating painted-ply seat, both employed cold-bent stove-enamelled welded steel rod. Ball feet reflected the Atomic style coming from America at the time. Many have since been replaced with rubber feet.

The Antelope Chair was called "the new Elizabethan" by trend forecasters trying to link it with the Queen's coronation. With seats originally painted in the Festival's choice of red, yellow, blue and grey, the Antelope had an upturned petticoat feel that really struck a chord with visitors. Chosen as "chair of the year" in 1951 by *Design* magazine, it was a progression from the revolutionary metal rocker that Race designed in 1948, inspired by an 1850s example of the Winfield metal rocking chair that he happened upon while sourcing metal to recycle. Race's Antelope Chair won a silver medal at the 1954 Milan Triennale and it has since become as iconic as the Eameses' Hang It All Coat Rack in terms of fifties design. It can be bought with an accompanying bench.

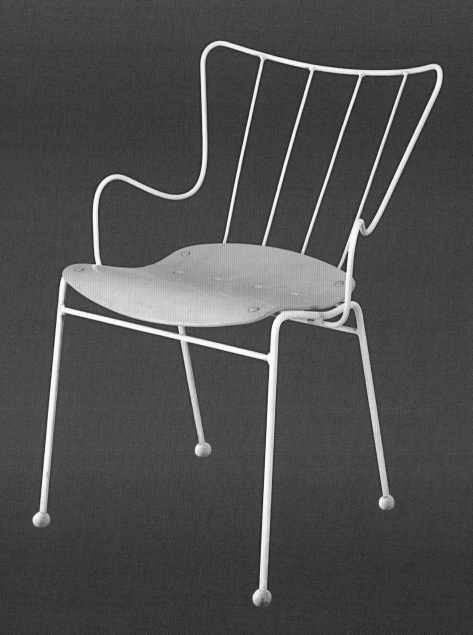

1951

41 The Upholstered Wire Chair, DKR (Dining K-Wire Shell, R-Wire Base/Rod Iron Base), Charles and Ray Eames, Herman Miller

Dressed like notes in a musical symphony, a cluster of DKRs is seen criss-crossing an image, co-created by Charles and Ray, with a prized wooden blackbird nestled in between the chairs, which, while now synonymous with the Eames brand, was carved by an unknown artist to use as a decoy bird while out shooting.

It all gets equally hazy when it comes to who designed which bit of which chair in the studio in Venice, California, and much debating goes on between fans of midcentury modern as to whether Harry Bertoia should get any DKR credit. Safe to say the duo were hands-on the whole way through the process and the final word was always Charles and Ray's. The Eameses brought out the DKR years after Bertoia left and a year before his Diamond Chair (page 104) was unveiled by Knoll. After a lawsuit ensued between Eames producer Herman Miller and Knoll (where the argument rested on the innovation of loose ends of wire bound at the edge by two thicker wires which soften the tips while stabilizing the shell), Herman Miller was awarded intellectual ownership of the copyright while Bertoia was forced to use a different method of finish with Knoll.

Harry Bertoia likely welded and soldered metal in the three years he worked at the office, 1943–46, and may have helped construct the three legged DCM, but it was the Eameses that developed the metal bases with modelmakers, and the Eameses who stamped and perfected the criss-cross pattern of steel wire inspired by shopping baskets on the DKR, well after he left the studio.

The fact the removable pads do not appear in the aforementioned photo shoot does not make them any less important. Removable upholstery pads were integral to the DKR's design as Charles and Ray were looking to create an easy-to-clean upholstered chair that was visually different from anything else. They first brought out pads in pin check cloth tweed (1951–52), then came the "Postman's Bag Tan" leather version. The bikini version came out of the Eameses' "best for the most for the least" principle. Removing everything that was not needed for comfort, they reduced the upholstery to its bare necessities and made it cheaper. The two-piece pad required less material and took less time to make. Always revisiting and improving on their work, Charles and Ray asked for the same premium material to be used for both face and backing of the pads in 1957.

The DKR, with its different base options of wood, metal rod or "Eiffel Tower", was awarded the Trail Blazers Award by the Home Fashions League of America in 1952, a year before Alexander Girard was brought in to expand the fabric range in 1953. He brought in hopsack and together with Ray came up with the super-rare Harlequin Pads, which were less popular and only available for two years according to Daniel Ostroff, author of *An Eames Anthology*, as, "They cost $10 more, and were perhaps too flashy for the time." After celebrated British architect Alison Smithson bought one of the early DKRs with crisp 'skivved' leather bikini pads, she described it as being like "a message of hope from another planet." [55]

1951

42 Element Chair, PK25, Poul Kjærholm, Fritz Hansen

Poul Kjærholm's PK25 or Element chair with its complex matt-chromed steel frame bent in a single piece and zigzagging upwards from the legs into the arms and around the back – continuously, without any visible joints or connections – looks too sophisticated to have been created by a student for his final graduation project.

Kjærholm's fascination with steel stemmed from classes at Copenhagen's famous School of Arts and Crafts where Sydney Opera House architect Jørn Utzon headed up the school's industrial design department at the time and Hans J. Wegner was supervisor in the furniture department. While Kjærholm learned the basics of cabinetmaking as a fifteen year old apprentice to a local master craftsman near to his home town of Oster Vra, the mix of the two mentors, with lectures from the great Kaare Klint, plus time spent in a blacksmith's workshop taught him about new technologies.

Spurred on by Klint, Kjærholm looked back to go forward in order to create furniture archetypes for the future. Here you see him inspired by Wegner's Flag Halyard Chair of 1950 but, unlike Wegner, he distils his design to the ultimate combination of two separate elements brought together to create one cohesive piece. Clarity was Kjaerholm's ultimate goal. Your eye is not disturbed as it moves around the PK25 because the chair's skeleton is shaped out of one piece of sheet steel, cut and then pressed. You can sense Kjaerholm playing with soft card at the design stage as you study the way the steel appears to have been pulled out like a Chinese lantern to the point where it creates the right

frame on which he can wrap the single piece of flag halyard. Every edge is smoothed so you cannot see cuts from the tools and the steel is sensitively brushed to avoid reflections that will disrupt the form of the frame.

The one piece of flag halyard woven back and forth in stripes with loops in between gives it an op art feel, allowing transparency in a room and highlighting Kjærholm's lightness of touch. Chairs are designed deliberately low to seemingly lift the ceiling height and allow the person first entering the room to feel the airiness of the interior. Kjaerholm's materials work so well together, as if they are in conversation, spurring each other on, and each material, whether it be rope, steel, marble, wood, cane or leather, is integral to the piece and plays an equal part.

After a successful stint in his workshop, Hans J. Wegner realized Kjærholm was far too talented to keep him in an assistant role and so he got his prize student a job at Fritz Hansen. The Danish manufacturer produced a limited run of the PK25 to start with and now use nylon inside their flag halyard to strengthen it. However Kjærholm left after a year for fear he was being eclipsed by Fritz Hansen's star performer Arne Jacobsen (page 100). He took a job as a professor at his old college before the entrepreneur Ejvind Kold Christensen, a man who had been instrumental in Wegner's early career, stepped in and championed Kjærholm on the advice of Wegner, and a new manufacturing company was formed. It would lead to a lifelong friendship and working partnership as well as some of the world's most covetable pieces of furniture.

1951

43 Lady Chair, Marco Zanuso, Ar-flex

Marco Zanuso believed the four years he spent serving in the navy surrounded by the latest in technology on ships during the Second World War taught him so much more than his architecture studies. One of a group of designers that helped transform a downtrodden and defeated post-war Italy into a dynamic design hub, Zanuso, along with Vico Magistretti and the Castiglioni brothers, showed the world how to party with design. A master at producing fun, colourful luxury pieces for the masses, he set about designing an armchair fit for a lady after experimenting with his rather more abstract Antropus (page 73). The revolutionary chair he developed with Pirelli's furniture offshoot Ar-flex would stand as a symbol of fifties styling for years to come.

> **"One could revolutionise not only the system of upholstery but also the structural manufacturing and formal potential... our prototypes acquired visually exciting and new contours... with industrial standards that were previously unimaginable."** [56]
>
> Marco Zanuso

When judges at Milan's 1951 Triennale went on to the Ar-flex stand they could not fail to be dazzled by the way Zanuso and his team of engineers had pushed upholstery to the limit for the Lady Chair. Poplar plywood armrests were bolted to a steel structure. Nastrocord strapping was employed instead of springs. Zanuso's chair had crowd-pleasing curves in all the right places as he sculpted his foam in varying thicknesses depending on how much pressure would be exerted on each area by the human body. Bright fabrics added Italian verve, while thin metal legs poking out at angles underneath gave the chair the delicate touch it needed.

Zanuso left with a well-deserved gold medal for his confident design that turned traditional methods of upholstery on their head. The first of his Triennale medals, Zanuso went on to win medal after medal and several Compasso d'Oro (the golden compass) too. Set up in 1954, Compasso d'Oro is the highest honour in Italian industrial design.

If you cannot find a vintage version of the most iconic of all his Lady Chairs, Cassina reissued the chair with its black and white check and matt basalt legs in 2015 and continue to produce it.

1951

44 Ant Chair, 3100, Arne Jacobsen, Fritz Hansen

Back in the early fifties, Poul Kjaerholm played devil's advocate with Søren Hansen, director of Fritz Hansen, by asking him to choose between his PKO plywood chair and Jacobsen's Ant. Hansen was not 100 per cent sure about Jacobsen's light, stackable chair at the time, with its nine layers of millimetre-thin ply, alternating between grains for strength. The veneer had a history of peeling, and its three legs – designed to allow space for more chairs and legs – could be a little unsteady if you leant too far to the left or right. But Jacobsen had already got the go-ahead from pharmaceutical company Novo, after he showed them his design while working on their new cafe extension. By the time Kjaerholm approached Hansen, the factory had a mould for Jacobsen's design and it would have been impractical for a director to give in to the demands of this young whippersnapper. Thankfully for Danish design, Kjaerholm had to keep true to the threat he had made to Hansen to leave if his demands were not met, sending him in a new design direction that would lead to some of the most beautiful chairs ever designed in fabric and steel.

The design for the Ant came out of Jacobsen's desire to improve upon the stacking potential of the wooden legged Portex – a chair fellow Danes Hvidt & Mølgaard designed for Fritz Hansen in 1944. Jacobsen was also enthralled by Michael Thonet's Parisian cafe stacking chairs. He bought an Eames bent-ply chair for his studio after seeing Eames' experiments with bentwood and Finn Juhl is even said to have compared his Ant with Eames' bent ply later at the formal presentation of the Ant Chair on 3 October 1952. The Danish architect had set the team to work on ideas as early as 1951 at his architectural studio, including a very young Verner Panton. But there was a problem with the veneer, so Jacobsen drew in curves where the wood had started peeling, taking the stress off the central back and giving it a narrower waist. He never intended for it to look like an ant – that was the name Modernist artist Gunnar Aagaard Andersen gave it [57]. Like all his chairs, the shape evolved as he smoothed out challenges. The Ant found its form in 1952 after ten moulding prototypes and was introduced in the autumn of 1952.

Novo ordered 200 chairs in 1952. Retail orders followed and the Ant became Denmark's first industrially mass-produced chair. Six "siblings" with different backrests appeared over the next two decades as plywood technology changed, the most popular being the Series 7 (page 122) which soon overtook the Ant Chair as Fritz Hansen's biggest seller. A four-legged Ant was not added to the collection until 1980, after Jacobsen had died – he was adamant they kept the three legs while he was still alive.

1952

"I based my work on a need: what chairs are needed? I found that people needed a new type of chair for the small kitchen dinettes that are found in most new building today, a little, light and inexpensive chair. At the same time, I made one that can also be used in lunchrooms, as a stacking chair. It can be stacked by inserting the chairs into one another, consequently saving both time and energy." [58]

Arne Jacobsen

45 Diamond Chair, 421LU, Harry Bertoia, Knoll Associates

In 1943 Charles and Ray Eames persuaded their friend Harry Bertoia, a quiet, unassuming man who made Ray's wedding ring and was a whizz with metal, to move to California and help develop their ply group. They had seen the Italian's experimental work first-hand at Cranbrook Academy while Bertoia was in charge of the metal studio, and wanted him as part of Eameses' dream team. He had already mastered a soldering tool, but Charles Eames sent him to learn welding at Santa Monica College. He created drawings and small models pertaining to an all-wire chair while working for Eames according to Celia Bertoia but it was his frustration with not receiving credit for his part in the design of the ply and metal DCM and his desire to do more art that led Bertoia to quit in 1946. A couple of years later, Florence Knoll, another friend from Cranbrook, took him on at Knoll Associates. With a monthly allowance and the freedom to develop his craft without constraint. "Bertoia began with Knoll in a ramshackle wood shop with no metal tools, then by 1951 moved into a separate shop with a few tools," [59] says Celia Bertoia. Knoll and Bertoia came up with the name Diamond Chair over the phone one day.

The stingray structure took two years to evolve with the help of Knoll Associates' Don Pettit and Bob Savage which meant that Bertoia was a year too late to avoid Charles and Ray Eames' first wire DKR chairs (page 94), designed in 1951, and a lawsuit ensued between Herman Miller and Knoll, with the Eames producer awarded intellectual ownership of the copyright and a patent for the technological innovation in metal over Knoll. "When he was first shown the Eames wire grid side chair around 1951 my father Harry Bertoia was very surprised. He thought his wire ideas stayed with him and not with Eames," says Celia Bertoia, adding, "Of course Eames was his employer and had a right to use his employees' ideas." Thankfully, after a bit of editing to the edges of the metal, the sales of Bertoia's chairs did not suffer – quite the opposite. Unlike Eames' patented double-wire edge, Bertoia chairs have one thicker single wire edge, where rods rise up and are cut at an angle. Each junction is soldered, welded and buffed with the edges of the wires tapered to give a smooth finishing touch.

"If you look at these chairs, they are mainly made of air. Space passes right through them," Bertoia remarked at the time, later adding, "I wanted my chairs to rotate, change with movement." [60] The series includes a small and large version of the Diamond Chair, while the Bird Chair has an extended back with its own matching ottoman footstool. The Asymmetric Chaise looks like a seal lying by the seashore. Bertoia also designed a bench, a children's chair and a bar stool as part of the series – all created for indoor and outdoor use, and produced in painted black metal, and later with black or white plastic coating as well as chrome.

Although upholstery seems to defeat Bertoia's original premise for transparent form, most vintage Diamond Chairs come with a thin leather cushion. Knoll's textile division also helped Bertoia design a cover (made of layers of fabric and sponge foam) with hooks that attach and pull the upholstery around the back of the diamond. The Diamond Chair was such an immediate favourite with designers, architects and homeowners that Bertoia was able to end his employment the same year he finished the designs and use the proceeds of the series to follow his dreams as a sculptor to great acclaim. The Diamond Chair has been in continuous production since 1952 and is still a bestseller for Knoll.

1952

"When the sum of $20,000 [for the chairs] was reached, I thought it was tremendous. It gave me wings... I felt just wonderful." [61]

Harry Bertoia

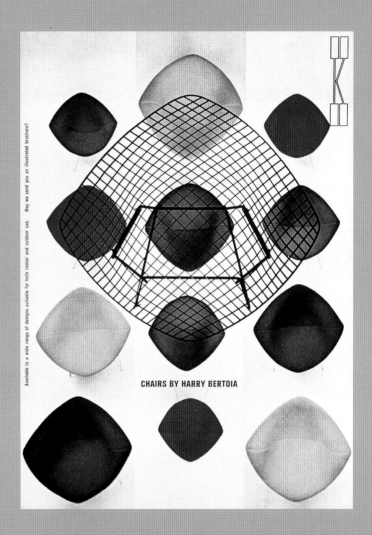

LEFT: Diamond Chair frames, stacked and waiting for assembly.

RIGHT: The poster by Knoll advertising Harry Bertoia's Diamond Chair, designed by Herbert Matter.

Reclining Chair, Robin Day, Hille

After the Second World War, television sets became more commonplace in people's homes – and what did you need with a television? A comfortable chair you could drift away in. UK designer Robin Day considered the Reclining Chair one of his most successful creations.

Designed the year he and his wife – the textile designer Lucienne Day – moved into a new home in Cheyne Walk, Day avoided cumbersome springs by using Pirelli rubber webbing, and kept to his mission to be able to see over and under a piece. Forever stripping away to the bare bones of furniture construction he kept the profile of the upholstery as narrow as possible – using

the smallest amount of foam needed to cover each section of the softwood structure, while taking shifting weight into consideration so as not to sacrifice comfort. Practicality, style and engineering: the Reclining Chair has it all.

Set at an angle to make you relax, the chair seems to float in its metal exoskeleton. The solid wood armrests have the added benefit of acting as a tray for your favourite brew. The head cushion's fabric straps allow for subtle adjustment. Rather than buttons or hooks that can cause damage to chairs over time the straps wrap over the top of the chair ending in small weights down the back. Never sacrificing beautiful details in his search for economy of materials and price showed how much Day cared about his customer. The chair appeared at the tenth Milan Triennale in 1954 in a shared exhibition space with Ernest Race alongside the Q Stak, 675 Chair (opposite) and Interplan range. Also on show were Lucienne Day's fabrics including "Spectators" which won the Gran Premio for textiles.

The chair was put back into production in 2012 by London design retailer twentytwentyone, and in 2015 ten of the UK's foremost designers including Sir Kenneth Grange and Margaret Howell paid tribute to the design by choosing contemporary fabrics for a special Robin Day Centenary Edition. Paula Day remembers her father's Reclining Chair in the living room at Cheyne Walk as a child in the fifties: "It was my father's easy chair. So he must have rated it highly both for looks and comfort." [62]

1952

675 Chair, Robin Day, Hille

Robin Day showed his prowess for combining moulded plywood with steel rod metal in his work throughout the Royal Festival Hall at the Festival of Britain in 1951. The 658 lounge chairs in the foyer made an extra-special impact, with wing-like plywood arms that looked like wooden birds floating above the sumptuous carpeted space. But by 1952 Day had found a more minimal lexicon as he overcame the technical constraints of the double bent-ply curve that he had used in his lounge and dining chairs at the Festival.

In the 675, Day pioneered a single twisting sweep of wood in an armrest and back. Steel rod legs were finished with the welded disc feet that was common in Day's fifties chairs. But this time the legs rose up to meet the sweeping armrest at an angle, bent under the arm and then, at a slightly lesser angle, down again at the back to give the chair the exceedingly strong structure that would make it a popular choice as an office, conference and dining chair. Conjuring up an even more lightweight look than he had achieved at the Festival of Britain, and with a modicum of materials, Day stuck to the economy that was still in force in the final year of the Utility Furniture scheme in Britain.

Moving away from the Eames and closer to Scandinavian influences such as Hans J. Wegner and Arne Jacobsen, smaller, lighter chairs worked better now people were working in high-rise offices and homes were becoming more sleek and minimal. In addition, companies like Hille were champing at the bit to export after the restrictions of the war years and furniture needed to be lighter for transportation. Thanks to Day, the 675 was a worthy contender when it came to representing Britain in the international battle of the chairs. Originals are highly collectable and new tweaked productions continue to inspire sales. After a Robin and Lucienne Day Foundation reissue by Case Furniture, a new version of the 675 Chair with flattened screws and a walnut back was awarded the Design Guild Mark by the Furniture Makers' Company in 2015.

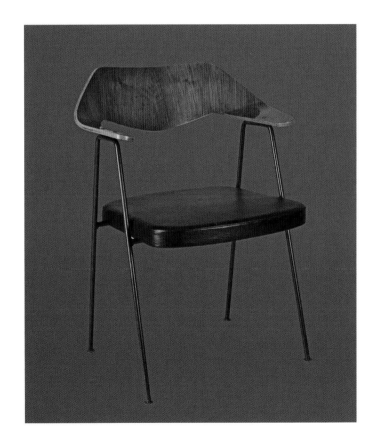

48 Casa del Sole Side Chair, Carlo Mollino, Ettore Canali and Apelli & Varesio

No one could accuse Turin's most famous designer Carlo Mollino of not living life to the full. A bachelor who put his dreams into action, conjuring up surreal furniture for the opulent buildings and interiors he designed for his clients, this brilliant architect with a background in engineering created his own car for Le Mans, performed stunt acrobatics as an amateur pilot and was a freemason who dabbled in the occult. Courting controversy as much as praise, more than 2,000 "private" polaroids with dancers and prostitutes posing both on and off his furniture in various states of dress and undress were discovered after his death in Casa Mollino, a secret apartment he kept in an uninhabited eighteenth-century house on a bank of the River Po in Turin.

Outside of his private life, Mollino was an accomplished skier and was commissioned to design a docking platform for a ski lift and set of serviced flats, the Casa del Sole, at the end of the forties. This nine-storey block of concrete apartments in the high alpine village of Cervinia was in direct contrast to the folksy chalets dotted around it. Had holidaymakers known back then that the simple rustic chairs they sat on at small tables by the sides of their bunk beds in Casa del Sole would reach more than $50,000 at auction today, they would have most likely sped off down the mountain with them strapped to their backs at the end of their holiday. There is little doubt the soft porn photographs he created, with models branded on the behind with his initials, or stretched around the most minimal of his chairs, added to their value.

"Although the chairs were originally designed for Mollino's Casa Cattaneo in 1953, the form was subsequently reprised and produced in serial quantities for the Casa del Sole complex the following year," according to Simon Andrews, International Specialist in Twentieth-Century Decorative Art and Design at Christie's. Inspiration came from studies Mollino made in the late thirties into Italo-Alpine rustic furniture. The chair got its other name of Pavia Chair from the Pavia restaurant, built in Cervinia a few years after the Casa del Sole, where they were used around matching rustic tables. The organic style of the chair, with its complex leg system distinguished by what carpenters call through-tenon joinery, is a world away from Mollino's usual sinewy Gaudí-esque shapes and has more of a tribal quality. Constructed from chestnut and oak, with a split sculpted back that pierces through the seat to settle on rear legs, the brass bolts and screws serve as much as a design feature as the nuts and bolts of the chair.

"Everything is permissible as long as it is fantastical." [63]

Carlo Mollino

1953

49 Teak and Cane Sofa, FD147, Peter Hvidt and Orla Mølgaard-Nielsen, France & Son

You will often hear the name France & Son bandied about at midcentury shows. Denmark's greatest manufacturer of teak furniture was founded by a demanding but generous Englishman, Charles France, who first decided to make "the Rolls Royce of furniture" while interned in a German concentration camp. He met Danish cabinetmaker Inger Daverkosen after he moved from the UK to Denmark and formed France & Daverkosen. But once his son James got to working age he set up a new company without Daverkosen, hiring several big names of the midcentury age and changing the name to France & Son.

Finn Juhl, Grete Jalk, Ole Wanscher, Peter Hvidt and Orla Mølgaard-Nielsen were just some of the designers to have France & Son patronage at a time when Danish design was conquering the world. Hvidt & Mølgaard were best known for Denmark's first stacking chair, the Portex, and their genius knock-down AX chair of 1947 (page 60). The respected architects and interior designers created lights for Kaare Klint (Klint taught Mølgaard-Nielsen at the Royal Danish Academy of Fine Arts) and furniture for A.J. Iversen, Jacob Kjær, Fritz Hansen and Søborg Furniture as well as France & Son.

Known for poaching staff from Fritz Hansen with the offer of generous pay packages, France & Son became famous for lightly sprung daybeds, sofas and lounge chairs. Marketed as a premium brand, Charles France refused to take on the Danish Furnituremakers' Quality Control label (which meant that you as a company had been accepted and paid to be part of the guild) saying, "France & Son would have little interest in joining such an association as no matter how elaborately their quality control was organized it would never reach the standard of control we have in our factory." [64]

With their speciality being teak, the company cornered the market after France devised a special saw in 1953 that could cut through teak without getting blunted by its high gum content. This three-seater teak framed sofa with its split-cane woven back was designed the same year as France & Son's new tungsten-carbide alloy saw. With its balance of cane, teak frame, steam-bent teak veneered arms and upholstered seats, it has a beautiful Arts and Crafts feel about it, and was created to be a piece of fine quality. Of particular note is the cane back and the front leg mortise join that is visible through the armrest. Hugely collectable, the whole beech frame can be completely dismantled with the cane rolled up for delivery, thanks to an ingenious system of metal joinery inserted inside the joints. The matching lounge chairs appear in Don Draper's office in the first series of *Mad Men*.

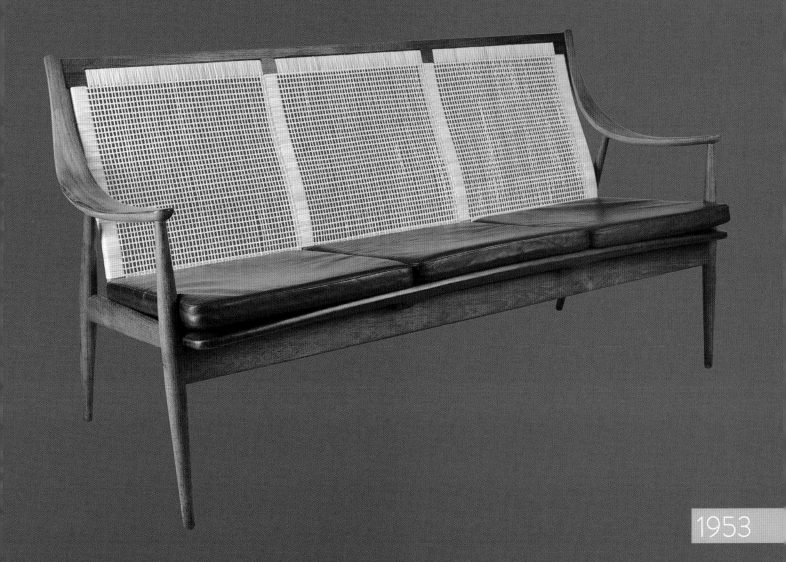

1953

50 Revolt Chair, Friso Kramer, De Cirkel

Had the founder of De Cirkel, Jan Schröfer, not read that he was about to embark on a project that would give him pleasure for years to come in his horoscope one morning, the history of Dutch design might have read very differently. Fired up by the prophecy, Schröfer suggested Friso Kramer design a chair that would eclipse the sales of Wim Rietveld's 116 chair for Gispen, offering him the equivalent of a million pound budget today.

Brought up during the Second World War, a time when life and death were closely interwoven, Kramer would help his parents forge papers and make life more bearable for the people they hid from the Nazis in their house. He took a humanitarian approach with his revolutionary chair too. Mixing the warmth and flexibility of the Eames' moulded plywood with the solid industrial aesthetic of Jean Prouvé's Standard he sounded the battle cry for a new Dutch chair that would answer the basic needs of people in an unpretentious, non-sentimental way.

Tubular Bauhaus-inspired chairs were looking tired and starting to creak, and the wooden ones knocked up quickly for the average family following the war were uncomfortable and prone to falling apart. Kramer's chair needed to be comfortable, so he moulded the seat and designed it to flex slightly so that the sitter would to be able to perch at different angles in it. He made space for movement in the armed version and found that by compressing, bending and welding cut-out shapes in sheet steel (more commonly used for the undercarriage of De Cirkel chairs) into a U shape he could make the strongest of chair legs that looked light and elegant with tapered styling.

The chair became very popular in schools and universities throughout Holland for its strength, comfort, economy and innovation, winning the Gold Medal at the Milan Triennale the year after its manufacture. Initially painted and varnished, it was later powder-coated. Material for the original seat and back remains undisclosed, although a paper and phenol mix was documented as being used in early productions. Kramer was forever tweaking his beloved chair. In collaboration with friend and competitor Wim Rietveld, the duo turned the Revolt into the Result with a quirkier V-topped kicked out leg in 1958. In 1967, office furniture company Ahrend merged with De Cirkel. By 1982 production of the original Revolt was discontinued, the official line being that the tool had worn out, although Kramer disputes this.

The Revolt was reintroduced in 1994 alongside one with a galvanized undercarriage for outdoors. In 2004 the chair got another update with a 1-centimetre (⅜-inch) higher seat and back introduced to reflect human growth. Beloved by architects, the original Revolt is seen as a defining Dutch design moment.

1953

51 Valet Chair, JH540, Hans J. Wegner, Johannes Hansen, 1951 (four-legged), 1953 (three-legged)

Any furniture designer worth their salt will tell you that only a supremely talented master craftsman would be able to create a piece like Hans J. Wegner's Valet. Any deviation in the finish where the dark wood inlay tapers into the lighter wood, and the whole back section would be wasted – a large piece of beautiful tree thrown into the offcuts bin. The violin section of the spine keeps shirt and/or jacket pristine. The seat hides a box for a man's necessities – his watch, wallet, keys or more likely his iPhone today. And when the seat is raised, it transforms into a hanger for your trousers.

The seeds for this ingenious idea were planted after a chat with designer Kay Bojesen and architecture professor Steen Eiler Rasmussen. Wegner was bemoaning to his friends about not being able to keep clothes he wanted to wear the next day pristine overnight. The name came from Asger Fischer, according to Wegner's daughter Marianne. Fischer was director of the famous Den Permanente at the time, a central Copenhagen gallery and shop that attracted connoisseurs in search of original workshop-made furniture and artisan pieces by leading Danish names.

First shown at the Museum of Arts and Crafts (now Designmuseum Danmark) in 1951, the Valet Chair was exhibited in the same room as a table designed by the Queen of Denmark. Her own husband, King Frederik IX, was so impressed with Wegner's idea and craftsmanship that he ordered one on the spot. But Wegner was not satisfied with the four legs he had originally designed – the two back ones stopped the front of a jacket hanging straight – so he left the King waiting for two years while he developed a three-legged version. Making the third leg an extension of the wood that creates hanger and back may have been a practical necessity but it also transformed it into the anthropomorphic icon we see today.

Wegner used pine with a teak inlay and teak seat for the King's piece in order to show a man used to luxury how a beautiful piece of furniture could be made from the simplest of materials. The King loved it so much that his office ordered more. Today the teak inlay is replaced by wenge and, in addition to the original pine and teak version, the chair is also produced in European cherry, oak or maple (with a matching European cherry seat, or a matching or contrasting seat in teak and wenge respectively). The maple version was suggested by head of PP Møbler Ejnar Pedersen when the company first took on the design in the mid-eighties. "You and your maple," sighed Wegner, "Do what you want". Pedersen's workshop went on to produce fifty mahogany Valet Chairs, fifty in maple and fifty in pine and teak and he was proud to announce that "After the fifty in maple sold out, we sold twenty in the mahogany and twenty in pine and teak." [65] Today oak is the most popular.

Wegner earned his name "master chair maker" after designing more than 500 chairs – out of which more than 100 went into production. This phenomenal portfolio of work has influenced so many of today's designers who cite Wegner as a huge inspiration, including Jasper Morrison, Tadao Ando and Konstantin Grcic.

1953

Rocking Stool, Isamu Noguchi, Knoll Associates

There was nothing Isamu Noguchi wanted more than to make sculpture useful. And he did it in the most extraordinary ways, which made him respected by so many artists, from Frida Kahlo and Diego Rivera (with whom he worked) to Arshile Gorky and Willem de Kooning.

While very few people know he designed Radio Nurse (one of the earliest baby monitors) or was best friends with the American architect, author and inventor Buckminster Fuller with whom he created the Dymaxion car, most of us would recognize his 1944 coffee table where two black sensuous wooden shapes hold up an oval glass top. You might still own his delicate washi paper-and-bamboo Akari Light Sculptures; remember the minimal stage sets he designed for Martha Graham and Merce Cunningham; have walked past the huge sculpture he created symbolizing the freedom of the press, commissioned for the Associated Press Building in New York's Rockefeller Center; or sat peacefully in one of his many meditative gardens. But did you know this son of a Japanese poet and American editor also designed a stool that rocks?

Anyone who likes to move a chair forward on to two legs while sitting on it will appreciate this tower of criss-crossed steel rods sandwiched between two wooden discs. Designed in 1954 and patented four years later, Noguchi's Rocking Stool now sits as comfortably with an Eames or Bertoia metal chair as it does with the sculptures of Henry Moore and Constantin Brancusi, with whom he spent a year as an assistant in the twenties. Inspired by African vernacular stools, the cunning addition of a concave bottom set the design apart. Noguchi originally wanted to try using the new plastic of the time but Hans Knoll insisted he stick to wood and metal and also design a small table. A full-size dining table appeared in 1957 with a cast-iron, black porcelain-finished foot. Early Noguchi stools now go for eye-watering prices at auction.

1954

Mezzadro, Achille and Pier Giacomo Castiglioni

As *Roman Holiday* premiered in cinemas, spinning tales of a bored princess escaping luxury for the simple life in Rome, Achille and Pier Giacomo Castiglioni were busy collecting unusual things and beginning experiments with iconic everyday objects in Milan. You get the feeling that life in the Castiglioni studio must have been hours of fun. Where else would you come up with an idea for a huge overhead light with a curve of steel and huge chunk of marble to anchor it (Arco) or a bright red plastic vacuum cleaner (Spalter)? Whatever you call them – early repurposers, witty upcyclers – their playful attitude translated into award after award for the Castiglioni brothers – who studied architecture but found there were not enough commissions in post-war Italy to keep practices in business – and so conjured up design marvels for the office and home instead.

Mezzadro is one of the brothers' most famous pieces. Like their earlier work Sella, a bicycle seat on a rocking rod, it was born out of the idea that some designs need little to no improvement, as Marcel Duchamp's "readymade" art had shown at the beginning of the century. Here you see a typical rustic tractor seat attached to a steel bow, similar to one that absorbs the jolts in tractors, using a bicycle wing nut. This is softened by finishing off the steel spring with an anchoring wooden foot, like the leg from a country-house chair turned on its side. Originally presented as part of an exhibit of the 150 found design objects the Castiglioni brothers picked up on their travels, it appeared simultaneously in a new industrial section at Milan's tenth Triennale and in a new exhibition at Villa Olmo in Como, "Colori e forme nella casa d'oggi" ("Colours and forms in the House today"). It did not receive its name Mezzadro, which in translation means "sharecropper", until Zanotta first produced the stool in 1971.

54 Coconut Chair, 5569, George Nelson, Herman Miller

Little did George Nelson know when he used Eero Saarinen's Kresge Auditorium as inspiration for the Coconut Chair that he would see his friend leaving the building in a coffin, his life cut short by a brain tumour, only six years later. The polymath, snapped up by Herman Miller founder D.J. De Pree as director after he saw Nelson's Storagewall showcased in *Life* magazine, rarely referred to Saarinen's building when it came to the Coconut. He preferred to compare his lounge chair to the tropical fibrous one-seeded drupe cut into pieces, with the colours reversed. "Coconut" had a better ring than Kresge Chair and Nelson had an innate knack for marketing: "If you can't afford advertising, focus on a few products that will get into all the magazines because they are odd or crazy," [66] he once said.

1955 was the year Disneyland opened on a former orange orchard in California and car tail fins came to dangerously sharp points. The angular Coconut Chair was a perfect fit for the Futurist style that was popping up across America in the upswept roofs and bold mix of materials of Googie architecture. Nelson and his associate George Mulhauser brought black and white together in a chair that echoed not only Saarinen's architecture but the work of conceptual artists Joan Miró and Alexander Calder.

At Plycraft, Mulhauser had proved himself both sculptor and engineer while producing stunning lounge chair designs in wood and leather. Nelson wanted to introduce new ways of sitting to popular culture as Saarinen had done with his 1946

Womb Chair (page 58), and he knew Mulhauser was his man. While Nelson brought harsher Modernist elements gleaned from designers and architects he admired to the design, Mulhauser added comfort without losing its sculptural qualities. It was a stunning collaboration.

Each edge of the chair looks the same size but the eye is deceived; the back is slightly longer, allowing for more comfort than an even-sided triangle would afford. A hard white shell is padded with a thick foam rubber cushion, upholstered in supple black vinyl and set on to a bent-steel, three-legged base with tough nylon glides. Add to that a person and the dynamic changes beautifully as the inviting armchair gives users the freedom to sit in countless positions and become part of the sculpture of the chair.

The shells most coveted by collectors were originally produced in steel, as seen here, with vinyl upholstery. The second generation of shell – in fibreglass-reinforced polyester – was influenced by Eames. Now the shell is made in plastic. The leg frame in bent and polished aluminium at Vitra goes back to the original design – at one point in the design genesis, steel tube legs were screwed singly on to the form, but proved too weak. Nelson also designed a footstool which looked rather clumsy and took away from the beautiful curve of the coconut shell. Today, the Coconut stands alone in its glory. It is upholstered in leather, has additional circulation holes on the underside and is produced by both Vitra and Herman Miller.

1955

55 Eames Lounge Chair, 670, and Ottoman, 671, Charles and Ray Eames, Herman Miller

First revealed on NBC's *Home* show presented by Arlene Francis, the Eameses' twentieth-century interpretation of the nineteenth-century English club chair appears in shadow behind a voile curtain. As the curtain lifts, the audience is introduced to a dramatic departure from the Eameses' post-war minimalism, followed by a film showing the construction and deconstruction of the chair. Two years of fascination and frustration, trial and error are distilled into just two minutes, giving the audience an instant connection to this unique chair with its three curved plywood shells. Headrest, backrest and seat forged originally from five layers of plywood, now seven, with two metal spines set on rubber spacers supporting the reclined rosewood-veneer. The chair was created as "a special refuge from the strains of modern living". [67] Designed to emit the "warm receptive look of a well-used first baseman's mitt", Charles and Ray specified sumptuous black cushions in glove leather filled with feather and down, which they changed to thicker leather after 200 chairs.

The story that the Herman Miller version set on an aluminium five-prong base was originally designed for Charles and Ray's friend Billy Wilder is not strictly true. The actor and film director hinted that he "would really appreciate an ultra, ultra, ultra comfortable modern lounge chair". [68] He sat in the 1944 prototype that inspired the 670 for *Life* magazine in 1950 and did get the 670 and its footstool as a birthday gift. But the chair was actually designed to fit into a luxury market taking shape with television a fixture in people's sitting rooms and the upper echelons of American society no longer striving for thrifty answers to domestic needs.

The Eameses used the chair to subtly turn America's sexual politics on its head. While one magazine shot a male model lounging with his feet up on the ottoman and a lady perched at the end, Ray Eames lies back in the lounge chair with her husband perched on the ottoman in an archive photo. In one Herman Miller advertisement, a grandmother is seen shelling peas on her porch from her 670. But there is no getting away from this hunk of a chair's macho appeal. Appearing in more Bond films than any other chair, fans of *Frasier* and *Iron Man* will doubtless remember it as the male character's choice of lounger.

It took two years to develop: the Eameses and staff model makers including Don Albinson and Parke Meek made countless changes including the construction of thirteen separate arms before it was rubber-stamped by the Eameses and sent to Herman Miller in 1956. It was over budget but as Eames Demetrios says when he quotes Billy Wilder, "No one ever went to see a movie because they heard it came in under budget." Success was sealed at the Milan Triennale in 1957 when it was awarded Gran Premio. It has been in production ever since. Herman Miller International co-owned by the Fehlbaums, now Vitra, started selling the chair and its footstool with a slightly more angular base designed by the Eameses in 1958 and there are some differences in the way cushions clip onto the shells. Needless to say, whether you favour the Vitra or Herman Miller version, it is hard to beat the 670 when it comes to being the ultimate television chair for successful comfort junkies. As a 1961 *Playboy* article suggested, it "sank the sitter into a voluptuous luxury that few mortals since Nero have known". [69]

1954-6

Midcentury geek's guide to spotting a real Eames Lounge Chair

Apart from the obvious sticker with the Herman Miller logo (black or silver) or white sticker with the Vitra name, the Eameses and their team wanted their beautiful creation to have a smooth, seamless look, which is why a genuine model is held together by rubber shock mounts glued and screwed to the wood under the cushions. Two aluminium posts connect the middle and top shells. Each post has three screws: one for the top and two for the middle shell. There are no visible screws or bolts in the veneered shell. If you lift up the cushion on the armrest you will see three hidden screws in an early model and two in more recent editions. It is here that the bottom and middle shells are held together. On a genuine Lounge Chair, a plastic backing is fixed to the plywood shells with hidden clips and rings rather than sewn or stapled upholstery.

• Series 1 Production: Silver circular clips, down cushions, boot glides to ottoman base, three (3) screws to armrests.

• Series 2 Production: Silver circular clips, down cushions, adjustable/screw glides to ottoman, two (2) screws to armrests.

• Series 3 Production: Long black clips, foam cushions, adjustable/screw glides to ottoman, two (2) screws to armrests.

• Series 4 Production: Any lounge produced after 1990. [70]

Soft leather cushions are sewn with a zip connecting them to the stiff plastic backing and filled with a mix of two foams or a mix of foam and duck down feathers. For the first three years of production, chairs had 100 per cent duck feather and down, but cushions became depleted after a couple of years of use and by 1960 the Eameses were offering duck feather and foam as well as all-foam options. Around 1971, Eames Lounge Chairs were made with a mix of foam and fibrefill. Pre-1971 cushion clips were circular and silver. Post 1971, you see longer and thinner black clips.

Labels help with dating the chair. The round disc was used at Herman Miller from 1956 to the 1970s. The black label was used from the 1970s into the 1990s. The latest editions have a silver label. Sometimes you will find paper labels giving vital information about where it was made and dating it under the seat cushions. Today the only authorized manufacturer of Eames products for Europe and the Middle East is Herman Miller International, now Vitra. In the US, the original manufacturer Herman Miller holds the licence.

The base of a genuine (vintage and modern) Eames Lounge Chair has five legs in a star pattern (the ottoman has four) in polished or chromed aluminium, or black with polished aluminium trim, with rounded, not square, ends to the legs. Fakes sometimes have four legs working off a spring or rocking mechanism. Eames lounge chairs sit at a 15-degree angle without moving into different reclining positions. They will bounce when you push back into them, with no squeaking or creaking, and they swivel 360 degrees. Top auction houses like Worthpoint in the USA believe the first 10 chairs or so were produced at the Eames Office in California with a super-rare swivel ottoman that appeared with the Eames Lounge Chair in a video aired on the Arlene Francis *Home* show in 1956. If you find a swivel ottoman with a bronze ring as part of the swivel mechanism, hold onto it. The first Herman Miller productions had push-on rubber boot glides on the feet of the ottoman, as the base had originally been taken from the side chair but customers complained that they kept losing the glides so screw-in glides to match the Eames Lounge Chair were brought in.

"The role of the architect or the designer is that of a very good, thoughtful, host, all of whose energy goes into trying to anticipate the needs of his guests." [71]

Charles Eames

56 Series 7 Chair, 3107, Arne Jacobsen, Fritz Hansen

Danish author, architect and lighting giant Poul Henningsen once said that Arne Jacobsen was so quick with the latest thing that you sometimes thought he was there before it happened. The architect and designer certainly felt comfortable with the contemporary art scene. Jacobsen loved the work of Alexander Calder – the sculptor who explored three-dimensional cut-out forms in space – and his series of stacking chairs in the fifties had a huge affinity with the cut-outs that artist Piet Mondrian made towards the end of his life in the forties.

After the success of the Ant (page 100), Fritz Hansen director Søren Hansen asked Jacobsen to come up with a chair with arms on it. Jacobsen's stackable chair series may have been inspired by the Eames but the form evolved from the lamination technique Søren Hansen, the grandson of the founder, Fritz Hansen, perfected throughout the thirties and forties and refined in his 1943 DAN chair. And, while initial attempts from 1955 look like a wooden version of his Swan Chair (page 136) on steel legs, Jacobsen soon realized he was going to have to come at this chair from a different angle – so he worked with Fritz Hansen engineers to make steel legs that joined the arms in a seamless motion instead. Marrying technology with an artistic component, he cut the back to fit the arms (rather than put the arms on afterwards as is often presumed) and this is how the 3107, an unobtrusive, stackable chair with an hourglass silhouette, came to be.

The most iconic chair in history became Fritz Hansen's licence to print money as Jacobsen and Hansen soon realized the Series 7 could work in almost any format: as an office chair with five wheels or in a later barstool version. A chair designed with a writing table attached was developed for schools, colleges and conference halls, as well as a version for churches, with additional bookshelves. Then there was the option of having 3107s covered in upholstery, including the duck-egg blue wool 3107s that appeared by floating rosewood writing desks in the sitting room of Jacobsen's 1960 architectural masterpiece, the SAS House.

The producer is still at great pains to keep its bestseller at the top of the chair charts with explorative videos on their website showing you exactly what a Fritz Hansen production should look like, from top to bottom, with nine hand-picked layers of veneer hiding two layers of Indian cotton for extra flexibility, put together using the best glues before being sanded and hand finished by their top brass craftspeople. One legendary YouTube video shows a member of the American team testing a Jacobsen 3107 next to two fakes for breakage. Both copies crack within seconds while the original flexes and bounces. Do not do this with the more delicate midcentury version which is slimmer and less durable.

Fritz Hansen's continued perfecting of the production technique has resulted in a chair with outstanding durability, albeit a little clunkier looking than Jacobsen's original pieces. Like the Ant, the Series 7, or Sevener, has become a classic thanks to the way it so easily adapts to different environments. The most copied chair in the history of Fritz Hansen, even the one Christine Keeler sits on in Lewis Morley's iconic photograph from the sixties was a fake.

1955

57 Butterfly Stool, Sori Yanagi, Tendo Mokko

Anyone who has ever had the chance to work with one of their heroes will understand the honour Sori Yanagi felt bestowed on him when asked to accompany Charlotte Perriand on her travels around Japan between 1940 and 1941. Appointed official advisor on industrial design to Japan's Ministry for Trade and Industry, Perriand, a master of the Modern movement, was set the task of advising the government on how to raise the standards of Japanese design. Yanagi's devotion to the Modernist cause made him invaluable to the French designer as he helped her create furniture and homeware that could be manufactured on Japanese soil and exported to the West, using local materials.

When the Second World War broke out, Perriand was exiled to Vietnam and Yanagi called to service. Ever devoted, he took Le Corbusier's book *La Ville Radieuse* with him to the Philippine front line. But the book proved too heavy to carry so he buried it in the jungle, never to be seen again. When Japan surrendered in 1945, the Allied forces looked to reconstruction. Buildings, as well as everything within, were needed to house the American occupation, and the designs were based on Western models.

The National Research Institute of Industrial Arts (NRIIA), established in Sendai in 1928, was approached to modernize industry and promote export. Designers like Yanagi were needed more than ever. Yanagi's father had founded the "Mingei" movement, which championed the beauty of everyday domestic objects, back in 1925 and his son stayed faithful to its roots, designing everything from teapots and ceramic cups to an automobile, cooking pot, toys and bridges throughout his career. He was called upon to design the Tokyo Olympic torch holder in 1964 and the Sapporo Winter Olympic cauldron and torch holder in 1972.

But it was his stool that would go on to win a gold medal at the Milan Triennale in 1957 for the beauty of its design and the way it bridged the worlds of Modernism and Japanese craft perfectly. At the time the Japanese sat cross-legged or knelt on tatami mats on the floor. Made from twin bent laminated plywood forms and held together by a brass stretcher, you can almost see a haiku scribe flicking the shapes up and out of each curve with his bamboo paintbrush as you look at it.

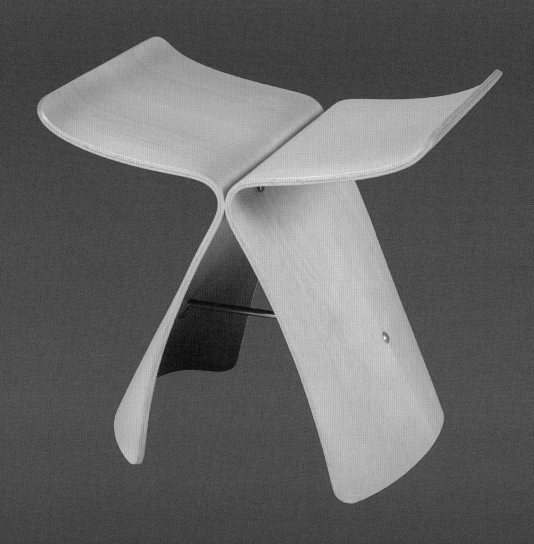

1956

PK22, Poul Kjærholm, E. Kold Christensen

Poul Kjærholm's work whispers rather than shouts. A natural who honed his craft first as an apprentice carpenter before shining at college, the Dane's lightness of touch with metal took midcentury design in a whole new direction. While his contemporaries mastered wood, he championed steel. Mixing it with leather, marble, cork, canvas and rope he studied the interplay of his furniture with light and space. "Steel's constructive potential is not the only thing that interests me," said the man who preferred to call himself a furniture architect. "The refraction of light on its surface is an important part of my artistic work. I consider steel a material with the same artistic merit as wood and leather." [72]

"Poul had a great talent. Nothing was difficult for him. It was child's play for him to design, to choose materials and use them correctly." [73]

Jørn Utzon

A huge fan of Piet Mondrian, Gerrit Rietveld and Mies van der Rohe, steel was Kjærholm's canvas, and leather, marble, cork and rope his paint. But every artist needs a benefactor, someone to champion them financially while allowing them complete freedom. When Danish furniture first started attracting press abroad, former sales manager for Carl Hansen, Ejvind Kold Christensen, brought Hans J. Wegner into the Carl Hansen & Søn fold and Wegner later returned the favour by suggesting Kold Christensen take his former student at the School of Arts and Crafts under his wing. Together Kold Christensen and Kjærholm developed thirteen types of furniture, while becoming lifelong friends. He advised Kjærholm

how best to construct furniture that could be easily disassembled for shipping and found master upholsterer Ivan Schlechter and talented metalsmith Herluf Poulsen to help push his ideas forward. With Poulsen's help, Kjærholm developed two low-slung ribs to carry the canvas on his early PK22 so as not to compromise comfort. He moved the steel to the sides and under the chair so it would not affect the sitter's back or neck the way it had on his PK25 (page 96). The legs on the PK22 were similar to the earlier chair, although the angle was dropped back slightly to allow for a more comfortable sitting position, similar to the Barcelona Chair by Mies van der Rohe. But instead of welding the metal, Kjærholm used machine screws which meant the PK22 could be flat-packed for delivery and put together by retailers with an Allen key.

Kjærholm wanted a material that aged as beautifully as the hand-finished chromed steel he had perfected with Poulsen, and luckily Schlechter had the best vegetable-tanned hides from Denmark's finest tannery Dominion Belting at his disposal. At first they used red or black Niger goatskin leather but switched to vegetable-tanned cowhide in 1957 – a choice Kjærholm did not feel totally comfortable with. "I am against dyed leather, especially black," he said. "But since people do not like spots, we are forced to use dye and varnish." [74]

As unfashionable as metal had become post-Bauhaus, Kjærholm's lightness of touch, the juxtaposition of soft leather with machine-age steel and fifty-fifty mixture of handcraft and industrial technology meant his lounge chair could not be ignored. In 1957 Kjærholm introduced a new wicker version of the PK22. He won the Grand Prix for his chair at the 1957 Milan Triennale and the prestigious Lunning prize soon after.

1956

59 Marshmallow Love Seat, 5670, George Nelson Associates, Herman Miller

A Jetsons-style future was promised for all during the Atomic age in design when the 'nuclear' dominated Western society. In the years between the forties and early sixties architecture, art, design and advertising saw atomic motifs appear in a multitude of ways. Considered by some as the earliest example of Pop furniture, the Marshmallow Love Seat, with its multicoloured vinyl cushions and varnished steel structure, used brightly coloured dots to portray atomic particles.

Although it is attributed to George Nelson, the Marshmallow Love Seat was actually designed by Irving Harper, design director at Nelson's own office, creator of the Herman Miller logo and the man behind most of George Nelson's clocks and advertising. The Marshmallow sprung out of a meeting with a salesman from a Long Island plastics company who showed Nelson and the team a product that he said could make 25 and 30-centimetre (10 and 12-inch) round cushions quickly and economically by putting a pre-sealed skin into a mould and injecting plastic into it. Nelson asked Harper to come up with a design, which he created in both a 10-inch and 12-inch disc version one weekend using a checkers set. He stuck the discs on a metal frame before drawing it up and set about creating a chair using eighteen "marshmallows" in an inventive pattern.

Unfortunately the plastics company could not actually fulfil their brief and the design turned out to be more expensive than Nelson first hoped. Harper had to get all the cushions made with a plywood back and added foam and upholstery. What was meant to be a budget chair became a luxury piece.

Because the chair and advertising were all designed in-house by Harper, and the model used to advertise the chair on Harper's posters was the company secretary, it did not cause Nelson too much financial distress and helped them market the George Nelson brand. But Harper was rather irked for not getting credit for what quickly became a museum piece. In an interview with Paul Makovsky for *Metropolis* magazine in 2001, Harper explains "...there always had to be one name associated with the work. We couldn't just spread it around." He goes on to say, "I'm grateful to George for what he did for me. While he was alive I made no demands whatsoever. But now that he's gone, whenever the Marshmallow Sofa is referred to as a 'George Nelson design' it sort of gets to me. I don't go out of my way to set things right, but if anybody asks me who designed it, I'm perfectly happy to tell them."

The smaller of the two Marshmallow Love Seats was reissued in 1999 as part of the Herman Miller for the Home line, and continues to be produced in limited numbers. Vitra also manufactures the chair under licence. Only 186 Marshmallows were produced between 1956 and 1961. Now highly sought after, the midcentury productions go for tens of thousands whenever they appear at auction.

1956

60 | DAF Swag Leg Armchair, George Nelson, Herman Miller

Herman Miller director, architect and designer George Nelson saw himself as something of a Renaissance artist. "In the best possible scenario the industrial designer brings together all the arts," he said in *Fortune* magazine. [75] Andy Warhol, Buckminster Fuller and Michael Graves all did projects with Nelson. But when he wanted to create gracefully curved machine-formed metal legs on his furniture, he called on an unknown graduate he had seen experimenting with a forging technique as a student when he lectured at the Pratt Institute in Brooklyn.

Charles Randolph Pollock impressed Nelson with a wire sculpture that he later presented to his idol as a gift. Pollock told Nelson he would like to work for him when he graduated. The war intervened,

and it was some time after that the young man went back to Nelson. Keen to produce a chair with a sculpted leg, Nelson was quick to hire Pollock for his metal skills and together they developed the DAF Swag Leg Armchair, now a coveted vintage design classic.

Nelson wanted the chair to be easy to assemble and disassemble so it could be shipped conveniently. Using a system called swaging – where the metal is tapered and bent by either pressing, hammering or force-feeding the metal using pressure through a die – Pollock was able to develop a system of swage moulds for Herman Miller to use in production, and the 16-gauge steel legs for Nelson's famous Swag Leg collection (originally called Swaged-Leg) were born. Nelson approached his friends Charles and Ray Eames for the seat to ask if he could use the patented moulded plastic they were working on, but instead of moulding it in one shell he created a separate seat and back. In one version the back and seat were fused together, while another offered an articulated back. The result was a sculptural shape that provided a bit of give and allowed the body to breathe, with the added comfort of space.

Placed at the Swag Leg Desk, its refined shape allowed visibility around and through the furniture, so as not to clutter a room. The series of ten pieces including the desk, two chairs, a bureau, dining and work tables, and even a small grandfather clock was ready for production by 1958. Nelson's mission to transform the look of home and workplace was complete.

1956

Lamino Easy Chair, Yngve Ekström, Swedese

Roughly translated as "taking coffee", the Swedes have a tradition called "*Fika*", that rather like the Danes' "*Hygge*" is all about chilling, a break taken from the daily grind, a time to shut out stresses and troubles and relax with friends. Usually, this break is conducted over the Swedes' favourite drink, with the most important ingredient being conversation. And what better chair to relax in with friends during the long cold Swedish winters than the Lamino?

Designed to give you that warm, fuzzy feeling of homecoming, the Lamino was selected in 1999 by the readers of the Swedish magazine *Sköna Hem* as the twentieth century's best Swedish furniture design. And you can see why. The beauty of this simple, comfortable chair is not only in its sinuous figure, its sling-like comfort or its temperature controlling surface. It also has a practical advantage for retailers in that it can be knocked down for export and comes ready to put together with an Allen key.

The glue-laminated bentwood and smooth curving armrests were very much in keeping with Scandinavian contemporaries Alvar Aalto and Bruno Mathsson, but no one had produced such a symbol of Scandinavians' love of warmth and comfort up until this point (although they had been throwing sheepskin over chairs and benches since Viking times).

After meticulous studies in sitting and the human body, extensive tweaks and a series of easy chairs with various names, Ekström, who had worked from the age of thirteen in the sawmill where his father turned wooden chairs, was able to merge comfort and laminated curve in this distinctive organic shape, with its beautiful split laminate arms, that is still made by skilled craftsmen at the factory in Vaggeryd, Småland, Sweden today. With his brother Jerker, they changed the name of the company from ESE to Swedese after Yngve visited the Salone Internazionale del Mobile in Milan for the first time and realized that they needed to promote their heritage, after spotting a Danish brand with the name Danese – Danish in Italian.

Be advised to buy the Lamino in leather if you have feral cats, as (in my experience) they love to scratch up the sheepskin, although the sheepskin version is the one that collectors tend to hanker after. Best bought with the matching ottoman.

1956

Tulip Chair, 151, Eero Saarinen, Knoll Associates

After the success of Saarinen's 70 series, which included the Womb Chair (page 58) and Model 72, Hans Knoll was keen to get Saarinen designing an additional collection, based on the commercial success of the first. Believing that he and Charles Eames may have been rather steered off course by plywood, following their original plan to create a structural total, Saarinen responded days later with the line, "I am really very enthusiastic about the whole idea... I have come up with an idea that I think will wipe Herman Miller off the map." [76] Like a couple of front row Grand Prix drivers, Eames (for Herman Miller) and Saarinen (for Knoll), the designers loved the thrill of cutting each other up with a headline-making design. Friends since Cranbrook Academy they collaborated on several projects, including a groundbreaking collection of moulded plywood chairs for the MOMA-sponsored 1940 Organic Design in Home Furnishings competition that was awarded first prize in all categories. Saarinen was itching to get ahead of the game again following his success with his Womb Chair for Knoll.

Destined to clear up what he called "the slum of legs", Saarinen's plan was to reinvent the base of the dining chair, creating it in one sleek piece – something that had not yet been achieved. Drawing on his early training as a sculptor, the ambidextrous Saarinen refined his design countless times, working with both hands, modifying the shape with clay again and again until he came up with curves he was happy with. Rigorous testing was applied as family and friends were made to act as guinea pigs in the dining room of the family home in Bloomfield Hills, Detroit. Had the technology been available at the time, Saarinen would have pipped Verner Panton at the post and made the whole chair in one piece of plastic, but the pedestal kept breaking. So, with the help of Knoll employee Don Petitt, Saarinen was forced to put the sculptural fibreglass shell seats on an aluminium stem with a fused plastic finish. The Tulip Chair, with (150) and without arms (151, seen here), remains part of a series of the most widely recognized furniture to date. It is certainly the collection that shouts "Knoll" as soon as anyone sees it. Saarinen designed his furniture to be democratic and without an individual dramatic statement. He saw furniture as architecture and refused to pander to consumer trends but, with the dawning of the space age, the Knoll Pedestal series became as ubiquitous in cool interiors of the fifties and sixties as Twiggy was to sixties fashion, becoming the go-to dining collection for its Jetson look – as well as for the space it afforded your knees.

Saarinen was never able to fulfil his dream of creating a one-legged chair in a single piece of plastic. Not long after the Tulip series was put into production, this consummate professional with a 365-day work ethic died suddenly from a brain tumour, midway through designing the TWA Flight Centre at JFK airport. Saarinen may not have finished his building, dubbed "The Grand Central of the jet age" by architect Robert A.M. Stern, or achieved his structural total, but he certainly reinvented the chair with his Tulip.

1956–7

Scandia Chair, Hans Brattrud, Hove Möbler

Eye-catching from the outset, it is hard to believe that Norway's most famous designer Hans Brattrud's stackable Scandia dining chair, with its laminated ribs rising up from chromed steel legs, was designed for his final year project. A startlingly brilliant design that his professors thought impossible to manufacture (such were the production limitations at the time) Brattrud went on to prove his teachers, architect Arne Korsmo and industrial designer Birger Dahl, wrong.

"When I first thought of the design in 1955–6, the fastest hardening glue had a setting time of about three hours," Hans Brattrud

told *Wallpaper* magazine in 2010. "This would not have allowed production on an industrial scale but, at a trade fair in Germany in 1958, I saw that hardening could be done by high-frequency electricity. I immediately realized that this technique would be useful in the production of my Scandia Chairs." Brattrud applied this technique to the production of the seemingly impossible chair and convinced a manufacturer to take it on. Thankfully for Norway, who are understandably proud of their designer export, Hove Möbler were forward thinking enough to invest in Brattrud's design, buy a generator and put the stackable chairs into mass production.

Available in two heights, Scandia Junior and Scandia Prince (the names given to the chair by current manufacturers Fjordfiesta), a row of screws holding a horizontal supporting piece of wood in three places on the chair are as much a part of the design as the carefully placed slats themselves. The satin chrome frame works in a continuum and fits up under the chair with plastic clips and screws. In 1959, the cabinetmaker-turned-designer went on to expand his Scandia range to include a Vipp Swivel Chair and a Senior Lounge Chair with optional Naugahyde seat padding, headrest and chromed steel legs. But nothing quite matched the popularity of the dining chair which, with its lower-backed counterpart, achieved great acclaim at exhibitions and fairs. In 1967 the Scandia Chair won Brattrud a gold medal for Design Excellence from the Norwegian Design Council and another gold medal in the Craft and Design hall at Germany's International Crafts Fair in Munich. After the Hove Möbler factory burned down in the 1970s, the Scandia series of chairs fell out of production until Fjordfiesta revived the brand with Brattrud's approval in 2009.

1956–7

The Ercol story is one of entrepreneurial tenacity, a tale of how a young Italian became successful in England in the twenties by creating a friendly environment full of local craftsmen with integrity. Erstwhile designer at Parker Knoll and lifelong friend of the Gommes of G Plan, Lucian Ercolani was one of the first of a small group of British furniture manufacturers to create a furniture brand after the Second World War.

Impressed by his delivering of thousands of tent pegs, munitions boxes and other supplies for wartime use, a representative of the Board of Trade offered Ercolani a contract to supply 100,000 low-cost chairs in 1944 as part of the Utility Furniture Scheme. After a year setting up the machines needed to produce the chairs quickly and efficiently, Ercol launched Britain's first production-line Windsor dining chair. One chair soon expanded into a collection, which was launched at the Britain Can Make It festival at the V&A museum in London in 1946. Relaunched at the Festival of Britain in 1951 as Ercol's Windsor Contemporary Furniture Family, the collection showed visitors how Britain could mix the latest in technology with superb craftsmanship in contemporary designs.

The Stacking Chair in Ercol's trademark beech and elm did not appear until six years later with a child's version fit for school use (seen here) with legs and back attached to the seat and the whole construction based around tapered and wedge-jointed components. The legs of these chairs go right through the seat and are sanded off flush with the seat, the wedged leg joint then adding to the design of the chair. The colours in the cut-out dots on the backs indicate the different sizes of chair. Some teachers placed children's names or class numbers in the dot to keep chairs in order. Comfort for children was provided with a curved back and sturdy moulded elm seat. Outward facing and tapered, the design of the legs meant chairs could stack vertically when not in use.

The Stacking Chair was one of the original designs by "the Old Man", as Ercolani was affectionately called. The smaller version of the Stacking Chair has become a much-loved and inexpensive collectable nursery chair for midcentury enthusiasts. Other pieces of note from early Ercol are the Love Seat and Butterfly Chair, which are often written about. There will always be a special place in our hearts for the Stacking Chair, which appeared in nursery and primary schools all over the UK during the fifties.

1957

65 Chandigarh Desk Chair, Pierre Jeanneret, Le Corbusier and Pierre Jeanneret

We all love to see treasures saved from destruction, but one story that has Modernists divided is the controversy that surrounds Pierre Jeanneret's furniture created for his cousin Le Corbusier's concrete city of Chandigarh. When Le Corbusier was commissioned to create a city for the modern age just north of New Delhi in India in the early fifties, Jeanneret was brought in to oversee it, as well as to work with local craftsmen designing everything from this desk and chair with its caned backrest and seat with straight arms raised on almost indestructible scissor legs to lamp posts and manhole covers.

By the eighties, the people working in the city's municipal offices had little desire for the old furniture and wanted the new metal and leather look they saw in magazines, so Jeanneret's furniture was piled up and left to rot, with scavengers carting pieces off to local auctions and junkyards for a few pennies. Thanks to the local administration's complete disregard for the importance of Le Corbusier and Jeanneret (and the fact that in choosing weather-resistant teak Jeanneret created furniture that survived outside through both the rainy season and supreme heat), Frenchman Eric Touchaleaume found it easy to buy and export a large amount of furniture he saw stockpiled in local Indian junkyards and at auctions.

Touchaleaume returned to Paris, restored the cane, polished up the teak and eventually got the pieces he brought back into mint condition. He then wrote a book, approached some prestigious galleries to showcase his treasures, and offered the furniture for sale through top auction houses. However it soon became apparent that Chandigarh was losing an important collection of original design and architecture. Jealousy set in as local residents found out that pieces were fetching tens of thousands of dollars abroad. But, while Touchaleaume believes he actually paid above market price and saved the furniture from being chopped up and used as firewood, news got around that he had looted Chandigarh. He was not on the list of scrap dealers registered with the Chandigarh College of Architecture (CCA), so was not officially allowed to buy unserviceable surplus items from their auctions. Yet somehow he managed to buy seventy-three pieces of furniture from the CCA on 21 September 1999, without being present during the auction and with no official agent to represent him, according to a piece in the Hindustan Times.

Dealers and collectors were not to blame, believes Kiran Joshi, professor of architecture at the CCA, who said in an article for the New York Times in 2008, "It is not the collectors who were the problem. The problem is our perception of heritage. We thought it was junk; our government thought it was junk." [77] City authorities have since ordered that no more furniture be auctioned off and prisoners in the local jail now restore any broken items that are left.

Pieces continue to be highly sought after by collectors, including art dealer Larry Gagosian and architect John Pawson who both own several pieces of Chandigarh furniture. And it is easy to see why. As part of Le Corbusier's legacy, the thing that makes Jeanneret's work so much more valuable than the beautiful simplicity of the pieces is the fascinating story behind them.

1957

66 Superleggera, 699, Gio Ponti, Figli di Amedeo Cassina

Who would have believed that Gio Ponti, a man who won the Italian military cross in the Second World War and was never ill a day in his life, could have been thought so delicate that his parents felt it necessary to send him to a girls' school. It turns out that the passionate workaholic architect, writer and designer who founded *Domus* magazine had more fight in him than the mighty blue marlin. But it was his mix of super strength and delicacy that really came to the fore when Cesare Cassina asked his friend to design a lightweight chair he could put into production.

Ponti was fascinated at the time by the Chiavari, a much loved antique chair that had become part of the vernacular of Italian furniture. Named after the Ligurian fishing village that still produces them, the Chiavari was designed by a cabinetmaking *campanino*, or bell ringer, called Giuseppe Gaetano Descalzi, who

came up with his chair after he was commissioned to rework some French Empire style chairs for the local marquis in 1807. Ponti wanted to strip Descalzi's Chiavari down to its bare essentials and make it his own, and he did it again and again until he got it right. He did not stop at designing a light, compact, inexpensive "chair-chair devoid of adjectives"; [78] he also reduced his chair, like a star chef in search of the perfect stock, to 1.7 kilograms (3³/₄ pounds) of perfection, continually slimming and strengthening, reinforcing and reducing.

Using super lightweight ash wood, Ponti employed a clever system of slotting individual struts firmly inside one another at different heights to give extra strength. He tipped the back of the seat for both comfort and durability and tapered the legs, making the top of them triangular, although they looked round from the front. By doing this he sliced more weight off the chair, without losing its durability, and added to the design when looking down at the seat. Finely balanced and so minimal, in keeping with the architect's own zen aesthetic, the result is a super-stable chair, designed to be lifted up with just one finger.

The Superleggera, the third of a Leggera series Ponti started designing in 1949, was so resilient it is said to have bounced without breaking when Ponti dropped it out of the second floor of Cassina's office for a publicity stunt.

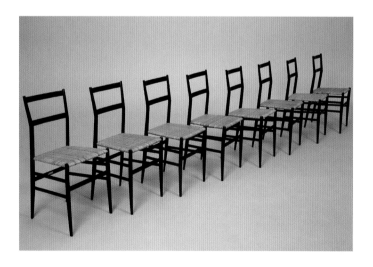

1957

Grand Prix, 4130, Arne Jacobsen, Fritz Hansen

Could it be the contrast of the graphic back with the gentle curve in its seat, or those beautifully crafted, sinuous, laminated beech legs that look like they might strut gracefully around the room at any minute? What is it that makes the Grand Prix a favourite with collectors? It would have taken guts to add a geometric shape to the top of a chair-back like that in the fifties but, as much as he loved to court the press, Arne Jacobsen never did anything without reason. Evolving from the Sevener (page 126) and Ant (page 100), which were inspired in part by the Eames' early experiments in ply, the shape strengthened the back, stopped the laminate lifting, acted as a perfect frame to set off the markings in the wood and worked magnificently in a room built in the round.

Jacobsen loved contrast. And just as his stark geometric buildings often contain a chorus of organic, curved furniture and circular staircases, the dichotomy of form in the 4130 (now numbered 3130) gave life to a chair of perfect geometry which worked in opposition to the walls of the circular Round House he completed for the manager of a local fish-smoking plant at Odden harbour on the island of Sjællands the same year. A set of Grand Prix chairs and table with matching legs once sat under the circular skylight in the dining room until they were sold by auction house Bruun Rasmussen in 2014. An upholstered version of the Grand Prix was introduced in the sixties. And while the wooden legs were later replaced with metal ones – as used on the 3107s to enable chairs to stack – wooden legs were reintroduced in 2014 after the Fritz Hansen team noted vintage all-wood Grand Prix being snapped up within minutes of the doors opening at reputable twentieth-century collectors fairs like Midcentury Modern in London.

The Grand Prix chair was first shown as the 4130 at the Spring Exhibition of Danish Arts and Crafts at the Danish Museum of Art & Design in Copenhagen in 1957, and got its name after it went on to win the most prestigious prize in furniture, the Grand Prix at the Triennale in Milan that year. One of the most coveted of dining room chairs by midcentury collectors, it shows Jacobsen diverting from his stacking programme to play with a more idiosyncratic chair, mixing his love of classicism, geometry, curve, functionality and craftsmanship into one glorious piece of design.

1957

Cherner Armchair, Norman Cherner, Plycraft

Anyone who owns a Cherner armchair knows the heart-opening feeling it gives you when you walk into a room. Hands down the sexiest plywood chair of all time, it resembles a musical note with its sleek curved arms – sculpted and steam-bent from a length of solid wood – and those veneered legs tapering into points. Fans of the chair will instantly spot the Cherner that Woody climbs on to in order to talk to Jessie in the villain's high-rise apartment in *Toy Story II*. But it is that Norman Rockwell image "The Artist at Work" with the Saturday *Evening Post*'s graphics man captured from behind that made this chair famous, back in 1961.

The result of the designer's passion for Bauhaus idealism and low-cost construction, this chair, laminated in graduated thicknesses, has legs as far as collectables go. Simon Andrews, head of Twentieth-century Decorative Art and Design at Christie's in London dubs it "one of the definitive expressions of American midcentury design, uniting innovative plywood-bending technologies with the bikini hour-glass silhouette and whiplash styling of 1950s American popular culture". [79] If its wasp waist and generous curves are not enough to make you weak at the knees, its story only adds to its allure. Imagine Cherner (seen above) walking past a Manhattan showroom and spotting his axed 1958 design in all its glory, six months after Plycraft founder Paul Goldman pronounced it too expensive to produce? See him walking into the showroom, turning the chair over and finding another name under the Plycraft production name – a name so fictitious it makes you want to spit out your tea. Goldman also occasionally used the nom de plume "Lou App" to include his Christian name backwards.

Quite why Goldman, a man who started out manufacturing sailboats in Lawrence, Massachusetts, and developed a moulded plywood tubing that was used by the US military during the Second World War, decided to change the name on the sticker under the chair to that of "Bernardo" and destroy his own reputation in the process is baffling. Cherner was a native of New York so he was bound to see what Goldman had done. This well-established architect had written numerous books, won awards and was friends with George Nelson, who recommended Cherner to Goldman after his own Pretzel Chair turned out to be too delicate. So with Nelson's witness testimony and the original drawings to hand, the Cherner-Goldman case was open-and-shut from the outset, with Cherner successfully suing Plycraft for monies owed and a commitment from the devious manufacturer to produce and pay for his design well into the early seventies.

Benjamin Cherner, who with brother Thomas took up the Cherner mantel after countless requests from architects and interior designers, remembers his father as "always drawing, the sketches that he routinely threw away were effortless and beautiful." [80] The brothers formed the Cherner Chair Company in 1999, which now distributes moulded plywood chairs, stools and tables in all manner of wood finishes and leather detailing, reissued from their father's original drawings and moulds.

1957-8

Egg Chair, 3316, Arne Jacobsen, Fritz Hansen
Swan Chair, 3320, Arne Jacobsen, Fritz Hansen

When Denmark was threatened with Nazi occupation in 1943, Arne Jacobsen, of Jewish Danish descent, packed a small bag and rowed from Denmark to Sweden across the Sound with wife Jonna and Danish lighting supremo Poul Henningsen. Jonna and Arne found work as textile designers, an experience that proved invaluable when Jacobsen moved from his wooden series to the upholstered chairs he created for his SAS House in Copenhagen that opened in 1960.

Originally built for SAS air travellers in transit, this model hotel for the jet age was called the first "design" hotel as Jacobsen insisted on designing everything from the grip on the window shade to the walls of living orchids in the indoor garden. Originally created with a palette of greens and blues, reflecting nature throughout, the hotel has since become an iconic landmark for lovers of Modernism. The most ardent check in to Room 606, where examples of Jacobsen's Egg and Drop Chairs, created at the dawning of this phenomenal project, can be seen upholstered in one of the many original natural colours that would have been seen in the bedrooms – duck-egg blue.

As much as Eero Saarinen's Womb Chair (page 58) kick-started the design process for a comfortable modern lounge chair, SAS chairs were technological innovations for their curviness. The Swan (overleaf), Egg, Drop and Giraffe Chairs were created to furnish specific rooms. Egg and Swan Sofas were also designed, but only three of the Egg Sofas were made as they proved far too expensive to produce. Legend has it that one even disappeared on the way to being installed in the SAS House.

Jacobsen loved using curved shapes as a contrast to the strict lines of his Functionalist buildings. Realizing he needed a low-backed lounge chair that would not ruin the line of his architecture from the outside, he designed the Swan with a bronze base to sit just under the windows of the Panorama Room, a bar with a view at the top of the hotel. The Swan was an evolution on from an earlier ply chair Jacobsen failed to get past the prototype stage that combined seat-back and arms in one continuous form. Without the arms it became the 3107 (page 122). The Egg, meanwhile, had to be taller to work with the proportions of the grand lobby area which was a huge 700 square metres (7,500 square feet) and incorporated a line of shops.

Knowing passengers would be constantly surrounded by the toing and froing of people going from reception to bar to bed, Jacobsen gave his lobby chair sides that could envelop the sitter when they wanted to read a book or newspaper, or have a snooze in transit. He also put his Egg Chair on a swivel mechanism so you could move it towards or away from fellow passengers as the mood took you. Designed to spin around effortlessly, early Egg Chairs, like the ones seen in the the lobby of SAS House, do not have the removable thin padded cushion or the tilt mechanism we see today.

Jacobsen perfected the sculpting of the Egg and Swan in his garage, working for hours on end moulding the plaster around chicken wire at weekends. In the book *Arne Jacobsen: Architect & Designer* [81], Poul Erik Tøjner and Kjeld Vindum explain how Jacobsen had to adjust the Egg's shape with model maker Sandor Perjesi as

1958

the plaster prototype looked too wide. They cut the finished model in half before surgically removing two centimetres. Jacobsen tried the chair out on everyone from the postman to his work colleagues before it was put into production.

All of the SAS chairs were made using a fibreglass shell in cold-cured foam rubber before being hand covered tightly in a natural fabric like wool or leather. Jacobsen wanted to ensure you could not pinch the fabric, so the leather had to be sculpted wet on to the chairs. There are no joins at all on the front in either fabric, except for at the very bottom of the chair in two lines either side and under the seat pad and then leading underneath in two curved shapes around the stand. Two hides or pieces are used: one for the front and one for the back. Both chairs are painstakingly hand-sewn, with the fabric stitch appearing around the outside edge rather than right on the edge to give it a better sculptural finish.

Floating above their star stands, both chairs are incredibly light for such large pieces. Look for aluminium bases cast in one piece if you want an earlier edition. Editions starting with a 5 will be the earliest as the date starts with the year first, followed by the number of the month, so an edition number 5910 will be from October 1959, for example. An upholstered footstool was also designed for the Egg with an aluminium base, although you will not find this in early photographs of the hotel or in Room 606 as it was designed more for domestic use.

"The primary factor is proportions. Proportions are what make the old Greek temples classic in their beauty. They are like huge blocks, from which the air has been literally hewn out between the columns." [82]

Arne Jacobsen

Cone Chair, Verner Panton, Plus-linje

Verner Panton, a jovial bearded Dane with a dog called Happy, looked at the world with a sense of childlike awe, enthusiastically embracing new materials and a bold colour palette. Conjuring up sculptural creations for the Pop age without compromising on quality, his work showed a man playing as passionately with design as a child would with his toys.

When the Cone Chair was first exhibited in the window of a furniture shop in New York, traffic police were called in to stop cars from swerving into each other as drivers became distracted by the chair's unusual cornet shape. This chair had no obvious back, no legs and was a grand departure from the wooden and cane furnishings seen in Danish homes at the time. Originally designed for Kom-igen (Come Again) – his parents' quirky new restaurant on his birth island of Fünen – Panton hoped some of his designs would attract attention, and they did. He used five different shades of red throughout the building he decorated for his father, creating red lacquered metal hanging lamps with reflectors connected by threads and dressing staff in a lighter shade of the same colour.

For the Cone Chair, Panton lightly padded a thin sheet-steel frame with polyurethane foam, then added Kvadrat upholstery and seat cushions. The semi-circular padded shell extended upwards across the back and armrests and tapered down into a point on a cross-shaped metal base on plastic glides. The heartfelt commission from his father paid off when Danish textile entrepreneur, Percy von Halling-Koch spotted the Cone Chair at the restaurant's opening and offered to put it into production. A Cone with a heart-shaped

back was produced the same year. At first Fritz Hansen wanted to manufacture the controversial chair and its matching stool as they were already producing Panton's Bachelor and Tivoli chairs, but after they pulled out, von Halling-Koch was given free rein to create Plus-linje, a new company created to make a star out of the Panton Cone.

The Cone caused even more controversy when in 1961 the Danish design magazine *Mobilia* let Panton drape his chairs with naked shop mannequins and models for a shoot. Sales were good and Panton produced a more transparent Wire Cone Chair with bent steel upholstered minimally with round leather pads in 1963.

1958

Hanging Egg Chair, Nanna and Jørgen Ditzel, R. Wengler

ABOVE: Dennie Ditzel in her parents' famous Hanging Egg Chair.

One evening in 1952 Danish husband-and-wife team Nanna and Jørgen Ditzel counted fifty furniture legs in their small sitting room and, thinking they could come up with a better seating arrangement if they worked vertically as well as horizontally, they designed their first domestic multi-level seating system. "My parents were very interested in using all dimensions of the room," remembers Dennie Ditzel. "I think the Hanging Egg Chair is a result of the same thinking." [83]

Four years later, in 1956, Nanna and Jørgen, along with the Finnish designer, sculptor and educator Timo Sarpaneva, were awarded the much-coveted Lunning Prize, founded by Frederik Lunning, owner of Georg Jensen Inc., New York. Presented annually to two outstanding Scandinavian brands, the prize gave young designers a chance to gain worldly experience and recognition by funding travel to places where winners could study and find inspiration in the decorative arts.

Nanna and Jørgen chose countries including Mexico and Greece, and on their return came up with a woven wicker line that reflected the indoor-outdoor living they had seen on their travels. It would evolve into the iconic Hanging Egg Chair they created with Robert Wengler, the most talented wicker man in Denmark, and later feature in many sixties fashion and interiors editorials, giving an expression to the new feeling of liberation amongst the younger generation. The Ditzels were not the only designers to have prototypes made in Wengler's workshop in Copenhagen. Arne Jacobsen and Kay Bojesen were also blessed with Wengler's magic touch with wicker. But no rattan piece hangs so beautifully, suspended from a simple chain, or has stood the test of time as much as Ditzel's glory piece with its beautifully moulded circular cushion.

The Ditzels were prolific in their output. Working across a gamut of materials with incredible ease, they played with fibreglass, foam and textiles and designed interiors, as well as furniture for both adults and children, and fabrics and jewellery for Georg Jensen. One of their most famous designs are still their rattan and wicker pieces, of which the Hanging Egg Chair is the most celebrated. Now produced by Sika-Design in Denmark, this beautiful, sculptural basket-weave egg is one of the most coveted collectables by interior designers and can be bought with a steel frame stand as well as the original chain design. Although Jørgen died young at the age of forty and Nanna later remarried, the first lady of Danish design was still designing up until a few months before her death at the age of 82 in June 2005.

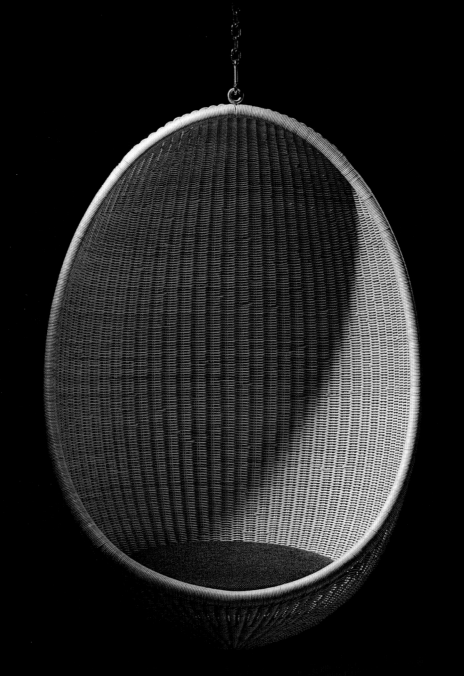

1959

Spanish Chair, 2226, Børge Mogensen, Fredericia Møbelfabrik

Børge Mogensen's name rarely crops up outside the world of collectors, designers and dealers and yet he is one of midcentury modern's most important proponents. Rather than expecting people to make their interiors fit his furniture, he designed furniture and shelving to fit a family's needs based on strict mathematical formulas. He called for high quality and an understanding of the best materials and, by improving and refining existing forms, like his teacher Kaare Klint before him, he led the way for more experimental designers to push design to its limit.

In character, Mogensen was not as strict as his work ethic led people to believe. One story goes that he would ply visitors to his studio with a good homemade dinner with beer and schnapps while his friend Hans J. Wegner preferred to give people buttermilk or tea. Friends from college, Mogensen and Wegner had very different approaches. Mogensen was rational, Wegner was intuitive.

But then came the Spanish Chair, a seat inspired by a very low, traditional, throne-like, Spanish officer's chair Mogensen spotted while on holiday in Andalucia. In his mind's eye he kept the broad armrests, removed the elaborate carvings, and brought in elements of the Hunting Chair he had designed a few years before. He fashioned a frame out of oak and cut a back and seat out of vegetable-tanned saddle leather, adding straps so the owner could tighten the hide as it expanded with use over time.

While there are elements of the rational, the chair arose from a flash of inspiration and went completely against the mood of the late fifties, when designers Arne Jacobsen and Verner Panton were starting to look at moulding plastic and upholstery into organic forms. Børge Mogensen instead went straight back to his beloved oak and leather from tanning house Tärnsjö Garveri to produce a chair he had fallen in love with, suggesting that perhaps he was a bit more intuitive and passionate than people gave him credit for.

1959

Time-Life Stool, Charles and Ray Eames, Herman Miller

Often left out of the credits and described rather unkindly in a 1969 PBS broadcast as sitting like "a delicious dumpling in a doll's dress", Ray Eames worked hard to be recognized as a serious designer in her own right. As one of artist Hans Hofmann's students in New York – where she was in the same class as the father of actor Robert de Niro – Ray Eames was active at the birth of abstract expressionism in America and later expanded to all manner of media, including sculpture, at Cranbrook Academy where she met future husband Charles Eames. "She had one of those minds that feasted on facts," according to design and architecture critic Esther McCoy. "Along with this was a sensibility that could transform facts into art." [84] Renowned for her super-creative whirling dervish work ethic, Ray would go from giving input on furniture, to sticking inspiration on boards, creating textiles and working together with Charles on films. Although the films and his painting show Charles with a lively sense of colour, he often deferred to Ray on colour as well as art direction. "I never gave up painting. I just changed my palette," Ray said. [85]

"She rejected solo credit because all their work was joint work. She also thought it would imply she had nothing to do with the rest. And I think she was right," says Charles' grandson Eames Demetrios, but Ray was very active on the Time-Life project and especially the trilogy of solid walnut stools for the lobby of the forty-eight storey office building which housed magazines *Time* and *Life*. Taking some inspiration from Africa, the stools looked like giant chess pieces dotted through the interior alongside Time-Life Lobby Chairs (page 154). People queued around the block to see America's darlings' latest interiors with murals by Josef Albers and Fritz Glarner. Designed to be multifunctional, the stools come in three different styles with concave ends that enabled them to be turned either way for use as seats, side tables or plant stands.

75 Time-Life Lobby Chair, ES108, Charles and Ray Eames, Herman Miller

In the midst of the Cold War, American Bobby Fischer is lined up to play Russia's Boris Spassky in the 1972 World Championship in Reykjavik – the chess equivalent of the prize fight of his life. The room is set up with two lightly upholstered wooden lounge chairs with a huge chess board between them specified by Fischer and flown in from England. But there is a problem. The chairs are uncomfortable. Like Salome calling for Moses' head on a plate, Fischer refuses to play until the Time-Life Lobby Chair with its 11.4-centimetre (4½-inch) deep foam cushion, adjustable seat height and tilt-swivel mechanism is flown in.

The Time-Life commission came a year after Charles Eames asked chairman Henry Luce if he could use photographs gratis from the company archive for a film they were putting together that depicted life in America for Russian visitors to the American National Exhibition in Moscow. Eames made good on his promise to return the favour the following year by agreeing to design the interiors of the ground floor of the newly built Time-Life building at the Rockefeller Center. Ensuring the place also became a showroom for Eames furniture, new chairs including the La Fonda were introduced for Time-Life's restaurant, as well as the Eameses' walnut stools (page 153). But it was the chair Eames employee Gordon Ashby had helped the Eameses to perfect, with three plump, buttoned leather cushions joined together with aluminium

side frames, that received the most adulation. This supremely comfortable chair with its adjustable seat height, tilt-swivel mechanism and five-star base, made available with the option of casters or glides, was catnip to Time-Life employees. After hearing they were disappearing from the lobby and heading upstairs in the lifts, Luce was forced to order chairs for every executive floor of the building.

But back to the match. After a slew of soul-destroying tactics from Fischer, including complaints about camera noise, orange juice not being cold enough and a change of rooms, the president of Iceland's Chess Federation, Gudmundur Thorarinsson, decides it would look better if Spassky and Fischer have the same chairs. Another Time-Life Lobby Chair is taken to JFK airport in a limousine, put aboard the first flight out at 19:30 on 11 July, to arrive in Reykjavik in time for the second day's play. However, once the chair is installed and Spassky has played a few wrong moves he starts to imagine the Americans have implanted something to invade his mind or expose him to radiation. You have to understand, it was the Cold War.

The match ends with Fischer snatching victory from the jaws of near-defeat, securing a huge psychological victory over Russia and the best bit of marketing Herman Miller could have hoped for.

1960

76 Mushroom Chair, 560, Pierre Paulin, Artifort

Pierre Paulin had his Eureka moment while discussing the inspiration for the Martingale Chair with one of Italy's most celebrated designers, Marco Zanuso. "I liked Marco Zanuso's Martingale but I studied the defects," he said afterwards. "The fabric was not elastic and the folds behind not elegant." [86] So he set about finding a material that would introduce even more sculpture to his chairs than his heroes Zanuso and Eero Saarinen had been able to achieve. He started experimenting with stretching jersey swimsuit fabrics over tubular steel sculptures upholstered with Pirelli latex foam rubber for the French branch of the Austrian bentwood company Thonet. Then he happened on a form that would catch the eye of Kho Liang Le, a Dutch-trained designer born in Indonesia to Chinese parents, who had been hired as "aesthetic consultant" for Dutch company Artifort.

Hoping to make his boss equally aware of Paulin's talent, Kho Liang Le invited the French designer to exhibit at a small furniture show at the company's new Maastricht showroom in 1958. It was here that Paulin met Theo Ruth, another of the designers showing, who would go on to help him realize his fantastical pieces for Artifort. The Mushroom came into being two years later. Cold-cured foam was sculpted on a steel skeleton consisting of three hoops in varying sizes for the back seat and base, with vertical supports to hold the hoops in their different positions, giving Paulin a strong frame over which he could stretch the fabric.

Paulin was not so lucky with his Tongue Chair, according to an article in one British newspaper. When he showed Artifort boss Harry Wagemans his prototype for this zigzag shaped chaise, the Dutchman needed a second opinion. "I had tried to appeal to the lifestyle of young people. They were into low-level living," Paulin told the *Independent*, "Then, in 1968, Harry's son had a party with friends from all over Europe and they loved the chairs." [87] Even though the Mushroom came first, the Tongue was too late to eclipse Olivier Mourgue's Djinn collection (page 168) which used super-flexible fabrics over foam in a similar low-level style to Paulin. To add insult to injury, people started lumping Paulin in with the Pop movement, a label the designer vehemently rejected.

Thankfully, Mourgue's overnight success did not deter people from seeing Paulin as a supreme artist and innovator. And while a commission inspired by Japanese tatami mats for Herman Miller was terminated after two years of research during the 1973 oil crisis, he lived to see a renaissance of his work at the turn of the twenty-first century with fashion designers Tom Ford, Azzedine Alaïa and Nicolas Ghesquière battling it out to secure vintage Ribbons, Orange Slices and modular sofa sequences. Since he passed away in 2009, Paulin's wife Maia and son Benjamin have been busy working with Louis Vuitton to relaunch the tatami-inspired Playing with Shapes collection, and the Centre Pompidou showed a major retrospective of his work in the summer of 2016.

"He never made works to be stars. He always made products intended to work well. He wanted to be a good designer and to be someone useful." [88]

Benjamin Paulin

1960

77 Panton Chair, Verner Panton, Vitra

Verner Panton's smooth tongue-shaped chair, a development on from his plywood S Chair of 1956, was inspired by a factory visit where he saw safety helmets and buckets injection-moulded in one piece. He started drawing chairs with no rear legs while a student at the Royal Academy of Art in Copenhagen and had a prototype ready by 1960. But it would be several years before he could find a manufacturer brave enough to produce it in plastic.

Without a relatively unknown company spotting its star potential it could have been designated to the elephant's graveyard of design. But Vitra, back then a fledgling Swiss family-owned interiors company (who had recently become European licensee for Herman Miller), was willing to take the risk and worked with Panton to develop his idea for seven years, just as plastic was coming of age and going through so many metamorphoses it was hard for designer and producer to keep up.

Panton and his partner Marianne Pherson-Oertenheim moved to Basel to begin a long collaboration with Vitra. Panton launched the Flying Chair at the Cologne Furniture Fair in 1964, and the world's first cantilevered chair made from a single piece of plastic, his Panton Chair, in 1967. Only just over 100, moulded from cold-pressed fibreglass reinforced polyester, were created after the chair's launch, despite rave reviews.

Vitra's first independently developed product was not ready for mass production until a new high-resilience polyurethane foam came to the market in 1968, produced by Bayer in Leverkusen, Germany. Vitra boldly produced it, varnished in seven vivid colours, and by 1970, the sexiest plastic chair ever designed had sealed its iconic status in a sequence of shots, its glossy red incarnation the focus of a fashion shoot for British fashion magazine *Nova* entitled "How to undress in front of your husband".

Production was halted in 1979 as it was found the chairs were becoming shabby with use but it was reintroduced as Panton Chair Classic in 1983. A more expensive, durable, polyurethane version was launched in the nineties and Kate Moss was photographed naked on it for the cover of British *Vogue* in 1995. However it was not until a year after Verner Panton's death in 1999 that Vitra was able to realize the designer's dream and hit the ground running with a mass-market, fourth series, recyclable coloured polypropylene Panton Chair.

1960–7

Who would have believed that Verner Panton and Arne Jacobsen actually once worked together?

When you look at the Visiona ship installations for the Cologne Furniture Fair (1968 and 1970), Spiegel's publishing headquarters in Hamburg (1969) or the Varna restaurant in Aarhus (1970), you might wonder quite what Arne Jacobsen and his strict work ethic would have made of Verner Panton's bright flights of futuristic fantasy. You might not know it but the ebullient young Dane worked at Jacobsen's office in the fifties. They would later come to share a mutual admiration, with Jacobsen praising him to his detractors and Panton saying, "The older I become the more respect I have for Arne Jacobsen, although our ways of thinking differ in many ways. When you consider everything that Arne Jacobsen achieved in many different fields you realize that he has no equal. Of course his skills were accompanied by talent, energy, economy and luck. And perhaps everything was a little too tidy. But I have never learned as much from anyone as I did from Arne Jacobsen, including the ability to feel uncertain and never give up." [89]

Two years of working for Jacobsen on challenging projects including the Ant Chair (1952) (page 100) while being dubbed "enfant terrible" was enough for this free spirit. Panton left to set up his own movable studio in a VW bus with fellow architect Hans Ove Barfod. He continued to make frequent work trips to different countries around Europe, immersing himself in the international design world, making contacts and shoring up commissions. By 1955 the first feature about Panton lauded him as "The Picasso of Designers" [90] although he would come to be associated more with the world of Pop art.

Bar Stool, Erik Buch, OD61, Oddense Maskinsnedkeri

You could say Danish midcentury designer Erik Buch's most famous work is the Bar Stool that launched a thousand copyists. It was a popular choice amongst Scandi enthusiasts a long time before it starred in Don and Megan's sixties apartment in *Mad Men*. Not just because of the lip that lifts seductively at the back keeping you firmly in your seat, or the legs that refuse to break no matter how much they get dropped or kicked. As the patina deepens these stools just get better and better with age.

Buch created over thirty successful designs during his career, but none so famous as his Bar Stools. The teak Bar Stools with the rosewood step are the model most dealers eye up. Teak is easier to repair than rosewood, takes a lick of Danish oil beautifully and develops a deep orangey brown colour over time. Rosewood can be harder to repair. Spot one with screws on the outside of the legs? It is most definitely a fake. The only screws you should see on a genuine Buch Bar Stool are bored deep into holes underneath the seat. The side bars will have a faint wiggly pattern, known as a finger-joint, where the wood curves up to meet the vertical legs and under the seat. The back and front bars will sit lower with a slightly curved rosewood step for your feet.

Interior designers Roman and Williams chose originals for the Viceroy Hotel rooftop bar in New York and to work in beautiful contrast with the cool steel of the bar at Japanese restaurant Izakaya in Amsterdam's Sir Albert Hotel. The more dedicated Buch fan might prefer to go the whole hog and source Buch's small stand-alone teak and glass bar with its bottle rack, glass-fronted cupboards and pull-out stainless steel bowls and cutting board – to match the stools in an office or domestic setting. No wonder Buch originally created vinyl for the seats of his Bar Stools. Cocktail hour in the sixties went on all day; at some point it was bound to get messy.

"It's not just what it looks like and feels like. Design is how it works." [91]

Steve Jobs

1961

G Plan Easy Chair, 6250R, Paul Conti, E. Gomme

You just have to look at the Chesterfield-style button studding and Googiesque wingback points to imagine the whisky swilling and cigar smoking that would have gone on in the most recognized British armchair of the sixties. G Plan designer Paul Conti[1] would have been pleasantly surprised when his wingback armchair not only appeared in all the British midcentury cult spy series – *The Saint, The Avengers, The Man from U.N.C.L.E.* – but was later requested in black vinyl to seat one of the most famous fictional villains of all time, Ernst Stavro Blofeld, Ian Fleming's super-scarred, pussy-stroking villain in the 1967 James Bond movie *You Only Live Twice*.

The company was formed in High Wycombe in 1898 by Ebenezer Gomme, a Primitive Methodist, but it was not until his grandson Donald Gomme oversaw a range of reasonably priced modern furniture for the entire house, which could be displayed in full room settings, bought piece by piece and collected over time, that G Plan came into being, in 1953. The Coronation of a very young Queen Elizabeth II the same year marked a fresh start and even though some rations were still in place, young Britons wanted to mark the new beginnings by throwing out the old and bringing in the new. Doris Gundry at British advertising agency J. Walter Thompson came up with the G Plan brand name and a flurry of marketing activity started, with an advertising push in glossy magazines, and showrooms dotted around the country. G Plan even had its own gallery at Vogue House off Hanover Square.

At the start of the sixties when the chair was launched, G Plan was the most famous furniture brand in Britain and the Gomme family were very rich indeed after a company flotation on the stock market.

Previously advertised as "The World's Most Comfortable Chair" and photographed with a matching footstool in a studio with prize fish on the wall, customers were given a choice of chrome or rosewood for the four-pronged stand or wheelbase on their G Plan Easy Chair. Its swivel mechanism borrowed from executive chairs of the time with a rocking and gliding motion thrown in – one suspects more to help older people get up and out of the chair than to help the Blofelds of the world hatch their evil masterplans.

1962

80 Corona Chair, EJ 5, Poul M. Volther, Erik Jørgensen

Danish designer Poul M. Volther, a man who went on to influence hundreds of young designers when he taught at the Danish Design School, was said to be so inspired by the elliptical shapes left by shadows in a time-lapse photograph of a solar eclipse that he named his Corona Chair after the halos. Russian astronaut Yuri Gagarin had just headed into outer space on his Vostok 1 mission, and Ham, a 17-kilogram (37-pound) chimpanzee, tested the Project Mercury capsule designed to carry US astronauts. The space race was on and with it came images of intergalactic travel.

Designed in 1961 with a wooden frame, the Corona Chair evolved from an idea Volther dreamed up in the drawing office of the Joint Danish Consumers' Association in 1953. Created to use a minimum of fabric and to utilize new foams available at the time, the rather more cumbersome looking Pyramid did not become a commercial success as the complex wooden ellipses and wood frame had to be constructed by hand. This also made the earliest designs of the Corona Chair far too expensive to have any hope of succeeding in a competitive market.

Volther met up with manufacturer Erik Jørgensen in 1964 to ask him to collaborate and the more famous metal Corona Chair came into being with its elegant brushed steel exoskeleton of two spines rising up to support steel backed oval pads filled with cold-cured polyurethane. Working to support the body in just the right places, the Corona Chair was a slow burner in Denmark when it was launched with its brushed-steel base. Jack Nicholson sitting on the chair playing a narcissistic bachelor expounding on every woman he had ever slept with in the film *Carnal Knowledge* did little to curb requests for the chair in the US but it proved expensive to export, which put off large orders from buyers.

What could have been the ultimate Bond chair did not get major commercial recognition until the nineties when it was relaunched in 1997 at the Scandinavian Furniture Fair at Bella Center in Copenhagen. This time it was a resounding success. Today, with its elliptical, blow-up cushions, it has reached iconic status, becoming Jørgensen's most successful item, with sales of almost 3,000 a year. Last seen televised in white in Roger Sterling's office for the hit TV series *Mad Men*, the Corona was also used as the official chair for the heads of state at the EU summit in Copenhagen in 2002.

1962

Elda Armchair, Joe Colombo, Comfort

In 1963 the Civil Rights Movement was at its height, reflected in Martin Luther King's "I have a dream" speech. The Vietnam War was gathering pace and the death of a much-loved president shot in Dallas in November added to the spirit of unrest and rebellion. While Big Pharma invented Valium to anaesthetize the pain, designers escaped into comfort. Eero Aarnio retreated to his Ball Chair (page 170) and as Yrjö Kukkapuro finalized the prototype of his Karuselli Lounge Chair in Scandinavia. Sergio Rodrigues slumped into the slouchy rosewood and leather Poltrona Moleca in Brazil. Joe Colombo headed for his wife's loving arms in Italy, dedicating his lush leather-clad preformed polyurethane-padded armchair surrounded by a lacquered moulded fibreglass shield to his beloved Elda.

You might remember the huge white bachelor-pad chair Haymitch retreats to in the Capitol's penthouse in *The Hunger Games*. Moulded like the bud of a tulip around the back, the front acts like a petal dropping down while the bottom rotates on a base mounted on a hidden ball bearing swivel. Designed to engulf a person, transporting them away in a space pod to another planet, Elda abandons the usual wooden frame for fibreglass-strengthened polyester in an armchair fit for Colombo's imagined house of the future. Using the boatbuilding material that shaped the Eames' most commercial chairs, and giving it the baseman's glove-comfort of their lounge chair from the fifties, Colombo came up with the perfect chair for space junkies to curl up in. One famous advertisement of the day showed him sitting in it, sucking on his pipe.

The former abstract artist turned architect inherited an electric cable factory in 1958 with his brother Gianni and used it as a studio to experiment with design. He loved jazz, skiing and fast cars and, believing he would die young, he produced an astounding oeuvre in a very short amount of time that has since inspired high-ticket designers including Marc Newson and Ross Lovegrove.

Before a heart attack at the age of forty-one he produced the first chair ever to be moulded in one material, the Universale (page 178), the much-loved Boby Trolley storage unit and the mobile Mini-Kitchen. But they are just a drop in the ocean when it comes to Colombo's award-winning innovations. He designed a watch with a case that flips up so you can see the face while driving and multipurpose modular living spaces with James Bond style gadgetry. "In the future, we'll carry telephones around with us in our pockets," he once told architect Gae Aulenti. [92] Imagine how much he could have achieved if he had lived another twenty to thirty years.

82 GJ Chair, Grete Jalk, Poul Jeppesen

Once referred to rather condescendingly as a fine example of "the strong weaker sex" by a critic at the Copenhagen Cabinetmakers' Guild Exhibition, Grete Jalk took the early plywood experiments of the Eames and Alvar Aalto to a whole new level. Imagine the early sixties. Plywood had fallen out of favour with the design establishment. Designers were hell-bent on creating chairs that could be mass produced in the new plastics, and then in comes a Dane, and a lady at that, whipping up a laminate chair with more sinuous curves than the design cognoscenti had ever seen. Jalk managed to create the illusion of a single piece of wood taken to breaking point with a multitude of backwards and forwards folds. In reality, two pieces of teak and pine laminate were bent on one plane, folded and double-bolted at the bottom of both sides, with folds in the laminate designed to strengthen the chair while allowing some flex too.

Disillusioned with her studies in philosophy and law, Jalk took up cabinetmaking with Karen Margrethe Conradsen before honing her craft under the watchful eye of Kaare Klint at the furniture school he founded at the Royal Danish Academy of Fine Arts. Testament to her talent she beat some of the great masters of the time, bagging first prize in the 1946 Cabinetmakers' Guild competition in Copenhagen the year she graduated.

Jalk would go on to become a regular at the Cabinetmakers' Guild. She designed and arranged numerous exhibitions while also editor of Danish furniture and interior design magazine *Mobilia* with Gunnar Bratvold from 1956 to 1962 and then again after his death from 1968 to 1974. Her four-volume tome about the work shown over forty years of Cabinetmakers' Exhibitions, *40 Years of Danish Furniture Design,* is a bible for furniture fans and a collectable in its own right.

But, as much as she was revered by her contemporaries, Jalk did not become recognized on an international scale until her He Chair and She Chair won first prize in a competition organized by London newspaper the *Daily Mail* in 1963. After the winning chairs were lost in a fire, Grete Jalk re-created the female of the chairs that would become her legacy – the GJ. Jalk's own small apartment in Copenhagen had one in the bedroom and two in the living room that sat with the matching nest of tables on a honeyed coir floor in front of a wall-mounted antique Yugoslavian rug. Although it was only ever manufactured in a run of about 300, the GJ continues to inspire designers. Lange Production in Denmark took on the manufacture of the chair in 2008 and now reissues this most coveted of all bent-ply chairs, desirable as much for its rarity as its extraordinary design.

1963

83 Djinn Chair, Olivier Mourgue, Airborne International

Midcentury fans love Stanley Kubrick's *2001: A Space Odyssey* as much for the furniture as the intense action. This 1968 film, written as a joint venture with Arthur C. Clarke, used strategic product placement to raise funds, inviting huge brands of the time including IBM, DuPont, Nikon and Kodak to sign up. Inspired by a living room that changed colour at the 1964 New York World's Fair, Kubrick instructed his team to commission the top interior and furniture designers of the sixties to create vision boards showing how they imagined their products might look in the year 2001 in return for exposure in the film. The hottest designers of the time, Arne Jacobsen, Eero Saarinen and George Nelson, were selected but nothing stands out quite as much in the film as the low-slung red chairs designed by a relative unknown.

Twenty-four year old Olivier Mourgue's organic chairs, inspired by Islamic mythological "genie" spirits, create an impressive silhouette along the corridor of the stark white Hilton Space Station as scientists discuss unusual goings on at US-occupied Clavius Base, the largest outpost on the moon. You can imagine these organic one-piece chairs morphing into something else given a change in room temperature or scene. Created from polyurethane foam-covered tubular steel with rubber webbing from Pirelli, and zips and stretch red jersey covers by Bernard Joliet, Kubrick wanted them to reflect the more relaxed meeting codes of the future. Even though others at the time, such as Verner Panton, Geoffrey Harcourt and surrealist painter Roberto Matta, were creating interesting seating systems out of similar fabrics, Pierre Paulin was particularly peeved at Mourgue for copying the techniques employed on his Mushroom (page 156) and Orange Slice Chairs. But even though he got the idea of stretching fabric over foam from the French designer, the shapes were all Mourgue's own.

"Things should have a short life." [93]

Olivier Morgue

Mourgue's brave Pop-inspired collection included a single and double-seated chair, an ottoman, daybed and chaise longue. Early productions can still be found, but if you want a true Mourgue collectable make sure the foam and fabric have not been replaced for safety reasons. And be wary of anyone touting original Djinn Chairs from the film. Afraid they might fall into the hands of lesser directors and devalue his sci-fi masterpiece, Kubrick destroyed the lot.

LEFT: A scene from *2001: A Space Odyssey* (1968).

1963

84 Ball Chair, Eero Aarnio, Asko Oy

Early sixties Russia pipped the States to the post in the Space Race when they sent Yuri Gagarin out on his Vostok 1 space mission on 12 April 1961. It was a moment that inspired a host of designers and a glut of films, in a decade that would end with America sending a man to the moon. Designed in 1963, manufactured in 1965 and introduced at the International Furniture Fair in Cologne 1966, Eero Aarnio's Ball Chair reflected the space-age optimism that pervaded the sixties. It was one of Aarnio's earliest experiments with plastic, at a time when he and other plastic pioneers Richard Schultz, Verner Panton and Joe Colombo were proving a force to be reckoned with in the field of synthetic furniture.

> ## "Spheres are everywhere in nature. It is the most universal form there is." [94]
>
> ### Eero Aarnio

Eero Aarnio was born in Helsinki in 1932. He studied at the Institute of Industrial Arts and graduated in interior architecture in 1957. After graduation Aarnio worked for designer Ilmari Tapiovaara before heading to Antti Nurmesniemi's studios and then the Asko furniture factory. Like many designs the Ball Chair, or Globe Chair, sprang from a desire for a much-needed chair in his own home. Aarnio knew he wanted to create something innovative, but it had to be large enough for him to fit into while also being able to fit through a door. He decided on a room-within-a-room design that would closet the sitter away from outside distractions. Set on a turning pedestal, it would allow the user to turn into or away from the room at a whim. Aarnio made the chair by covering a plywood body mould with wet paper and laminating the surface with fibreglass, similar to the way you would create a glider fuselage or wing. He rubbed down the outside, removed the mould from the inside, added a stabilizing metal ring, upholstery and stand. He even installed a red telephone on the inside wall of his own personal chair.

When two managers from the kitchen and laundry appliance company Asko visited Aarnio about other designs, they were so impressed by the Ball Chair that they asked if they could approach their MD to put it into production. The *New York Times* declared it one of "the most comfortable forms to hold the human body" [95]. It became the ultimate baddie's chair as the centrepiece in Number Two's control room in cult British science-fiction series *The Prisoner* and sat centre stage in the window of Mary Quant's London shop surrounded by her Mod designs.

Aarnio went on to design other much-loved pieces in 1968 including two indoor-outdoor chairs: a hanging Bubble Chair made of Lucite, and his Pastil. Recently, Aarnio replaced fibreglass with safer types of plastic. His Puppy Stool sparked his love for toys and kids' furniture and he continues to create new designs for both adults and children.

1963

85 Executive Chair, Charles Pollock, Knoll & Associates

This designer engineer who once worked on Chrysler's assembly line in Detroit was certainly not into design for the money. Chairs for him were sculptures for the soul. But being left out of the credits when you have put your all into a project can eat away at you. With barely a dollar to his name, Pollock left George Nelson's studio to open his own office in Brooklyn after the Swag Leg collection (page 134) he designed with Nelson got worldwide attention, with no mention of Pollock's input.

Pollock set about making models and full-scale prototypes out of plumbing unearthed from an abandoned basement and did what burgeoning designers did in New York during the midcentury years: he got in contact with the equivalent of a top brass director in Hollywood, design legend Florence Knoll. The most powerful woman in furniture production had turned him down again and again, but Pollock refused to give up and went to the company she had headed up since the death of her husband Hans Knoll (in a car crash), armed with a prototype of his lounge chair. Failing to spot the Knoll & Associates' director as she was coming out of a lift, he literally bowled her over with his chair.

You would think that Knoll would have sent him straight back down in the lift, but senior designer at the time Vincent Cafiero had seen him mentioned in a major article in *Interiors* magazine a few months before and reminded Knoll that Pollock was no freshman. They had a potential star on their hands. Pollock received $20 for

rent, a development allowance and the legendary Don Pettit to work with, a designer who had swapped George Nelson for Knoll years earlier.

After five years at Knoll, where he became so financially desperate he had to divert electricity from a chemist in his building to supply his studio, Pollock unveiled what would become one of the bestselling office chairs of all time. Simple to put together, and even simpler to break down, the beauty of the chair lies in its patented metal rim frame which not only protects the edges of the chair, but also makes the leather seat look like a sumptuous soft filling inside its curved polypropylene shell. Available in a variety of upholstery options, not to mention different shell colours, this softer look for executives quickly became a visual symbol of the modern American workplace.

The Executive Chair or Pollock Chair still meets the same exacting specifications as when it was finalized by Pollock and Knoll in 1963. You can choose to have it with or without arms, wheels, 360-degree swivel, pneumatic height adjustment and tilt functionality. If you have ever seen the film *Catch Me If You Can* you may remember the FBI office filled with the chairs. *Mad Men* fans will recall Ted Chaough, Don Draper's adversary in season four, described by Draper as "a fly I keep swatting away," sitting in the low-backed Executive Chair suggesting that he, like Pollock with Nelson, was better than he had yet been given credit for.

"It starts as a thought, and then becomes an idea, something I might think about for years. When the time is right, I express it on paper, usually as a simple line in space. Finally, it takes shape." [96]

Charles Pollock

1963

86 40/4, David Rowland, General Fireproofing Co.

Back in the fifties the standard requirement from most design firms was for new designer employees to sign away all patentable rights for a dollar. [1] Refuse to sign, as David Rowland chose to do, and you would be frozen out of the job. Since a chair takes at least six months to build, the costs were tough on anyone going it alone, so producers had designers over a barrel. Suffer the financial consequences in design Siberia – or sign away your rights to your best graduation ideas.

After serving as a pilot in the United States Air Force in the Second World War, where he made twenty-two combat missions over Nazi occupied territory while stationed in England, [2] Rowland, a lifelong Christian Scientist with a motto "do the most with the least" came up with his guest chair. "At that time, there were beastly uncomfortable seats in the cockpits of the planes we flew. And during the many campaigns I was on, some lasting up to twelve hours, I promised myself that if I survived I would dedicate my life to the creation of comfortable and ergonomically correct seating. Once the war was over, I started my own peaceful mission. After years of research, sketches and prototypes, I finally had the light, strong and super-ergonomic chair, which is now known around the world as the stacking chair 40/4." [97]

At first none of the architectural practices he approached would make concessions for this Cranbrook Academy student who kick-started his love of design on a summer course in basic Bauhaus design with Bauhaus master László Moholy-Nagy at the tender age of sixteen. But he eventually found an industrial engineer who didn't need him to sign away his rights, Norman Bel Geddes. While he created architectural renderings for the theatrical and industrial designer, he honed and perfected the wafer-thin stackable chair with its sculpted ply seat and back, until it was not only ergonomically correct and beautiful to look at from every angle, but could also be stacked up to forty chairs high in the space of 4 feet in a very short amount of time – hence the name. Following rejection after rejection from people who remained unconvinced that such a lightweight chair would hold out, a friend got him an interview with Davis Allen, one of the senior designers in the interiors section of Skidmore, Owings & Merrill. Unbeknown to Rowland or his friend, this respected architectural firm in New York had won a commission for a university campus in Chicago that needed 17, 000 chairs. Allen put Rowland on to General Fireproofing Co. in Youngstown, Ohio, and they signed a fair licence agreement which would see the manufacturer invest money and engineering talent into the creation of the 40/4 in both plywood and steel and plastic and steel.

After years of rebuffs, the chair became an overnight sensation in the US and abroad. It snapped up the Grand Prix at the Milan Triennale in 1964, a Gold Medal for Furniture from the Austrian government, and the American Institute of Interior Designers First Prize. Everyone wanted the 40/4, from the Pompidou Centre to St Paul's Cathedral, where it was used for the wedding of Prince Charles and Diana. It is still the go-to stacking chair for large interior events, museums and cultural centres around the world. Unsurpassed in terms of engineering, the chair has been in continuous production since Skidmore, Owings & Merrill first took the plunge, selling millions around the world over five decades. Now produced by Howe, the 40/4 chair family expanded before Rowland's death in 2010 to include an outdoor chair, armchair, lounge chair, bar stool, counter chair and chair with a swivel base. Long may this king of stackers reign.

1963–4

87 Big Tulip Armchair, F545, Pierre Paulin, Artifort

Paulin thought in three dimensions. He originally trained as a sculptor, inspired in part by his uncle, the sculptor Frédy Stoll, until he injured a tendon in a fight which caused him paralysis in his right hand. "I could think up a shape and make it spin in my head like a sculptor or an architect would," he said. "I made the most of that gift." [98]

Artifort needed more pieces to complement the range Paulin had already produced, and in 1965 the bold French designer came up with the Dutch company's future bread and butter: the Little Tulip for dining and the Big Tulip Armchair for lounging, which immediately became bestsellers for Artifort. Sections of the Big Tulip were moulded in Paulin's sculptural style but the idea of a metal exoskeleton was new for Paulin. It allowed different segments on a crossbar to be lifted up off the floor and given space to float –

as Poul Volther's Corona (page 164) with its lightly padded leather ellipses had done over in Denmark.

"I do not create. I invent, I arrange, I design... even the term designer, which used to have real meaning, has been so misused that it has become a really sad thing." [99]

Pierre Paulin

Paulin was a perfectionist in everything he produced, with every junction and seam hidden and polished off, and no screw or bonding line in sight. Like Danish master Finn Juhl, he leapfrogged convention and usual practice, confident that Artifort's chief designer and engineer Theo Ruth would be able to make his designs work. Had he been too bogged down by the practicalities, his designs would have suffered.

Although the general public found his work too expensive, Paulin became a designer for the elite in his home country after Monsieur and Madame Pompidou discovered his work in the mid-sixties in an exhibition at MOMA. The French President and his wife asked him to decorate their private apartments at the Elysée Palace, previously dubbed a "house of sadness" by Madame Pompidou. The makeover included painted aluminium walls and colourful carpets by the Parisian-based Israeli artist Yaacov Agam. Other rich benefactors followed.

LEFT: Pierre Paulin (and model) sitting in his Tulip Armchair.

1965

88 Universale Chair, 4860, Joe Colombo, Kartell

If you were asked to name one designer who sums up the pioneering spirit of the sixties better than any other it would have to be Joe Colombo. The man who made televisions retract into the ceiling, enclosed minibars in moving walls, built climate-controlled sleeping pods and envisioned the freelance work environment the way it is today could put his hand to anything. He even came up with ideas for a subterranean nuclear city.

Following on from his Elda Armchair (page 165), Colombo designed and perfected the first all-plastic chair to be injection moulded from a single material and sold commercially. The Universale pipped Verner Panton's Panton Chair (page 158) to the post. Originally designed in die-cast aluminium, after two years of experimentation and research with the Kartell factory Colombo shifted to the oil-based ABS plastic that Lego hopes to ditch by 2030. After initial designs faded, Kartell encouraged Colombo to change to nylon and then injection-moulded polypropylene. Lighter, stronger and more resistant to colour changes, "It never ages, never breaks, can be thrown out the window, left outside, immersed in water, transported to the North Pole or the desert, and it will always look like new" said an advertising slogan at the time. [100]

Reissued in 1979 as the 4867, the Universale was stackable, easy to clean and a doddle to move, with the hole in its back working as a handle. Detachable legs were available in different lengths so the height of the chair could be adjusted for use as a side chair, dining chair or bar stool, and were also finished with a tiny slice of plastic that acted as a foot and slotted in subtly underneath, making it easy to replace as it wore down. Colombo's Universale helped former plastics lab Kartell raise the profile of plastic throughout the world, taking it from the thrifty to the sublime.

1965

Martin Visser believed he was a better collector than designer. The chief curator at Museum Boijmans van Beuningen in Rotterdam from 1978–83 and owner of a much feted personal art collection, Visser believed Friso Kramer was a much better designer and saw his own furniture as a means to an end.[101] And yet he sits beside Gerrit Rietveld and Kramer as one of Holland's most lauded furniture makers, responsible for one of the Netherland's most iconic chairs, not to mention the perfect wooden art gallery bench (BZ72) and the most minimal of modern sofa beds (BR02).

The house Gerrit Rietveld designed for Visser in 1954 has become home to works by Anselm Kiefer, Sigmar Polke, Piero Manzoni and Keith Haring as well as a wealth of Dutch artists. Here you can also see the part-Functionalist part-Bauhaus inspired furniture Visser conceived for 't Spectrum in Bergeijk while he was head designer, and his SZ series that is even more abstract than his taste in art. The SZ series strips furniture back to its most minimal and takes metal to the edge of perfection. Rather than bending the metal tubing that makes up the skeleton, Visser mixed engineering with work by hand. He cut and welded the metal on his chairs so precisely as to befuddle your instinct and leave you totally confused as to how he could create such stark angular shapes. In a careful honing of craft, matt chrome-plated metal is set off by textured rattan in the SZ01 (pictured) while leather is thoughtfully belted around the underside and back of the SZ02 so that you can pull it in to stop the natural sagging that happens to the material over time.

Stretching technique to the limit with learned engineering skills and an honest use of materials, Visser was able to make his intricately crafted furniture look effortless. Although he himself admitted to being very much inspired by Gerrit Rietveld, Le Corbusier and Marcel Breuer,[102] Visser was a much more talented designer than he allowed himself credit for.

1965

90 Platner Armchair, Warren Platner, Knoll International

If you want a chair that exudes modern glamour, one with all the curves and padding in the right places, a Marilyn Monroe of chairs, look no further than architect, interior and product designer Warren Platner.

You might remember seeing these chairs with matching tables near the end of the 2008 film *Quantum of Solace* where Dominic Greene and James Bond fight it out. Bond runs through the dining space as it blows up, leaving a shattered group of glass tables and metal and leather chairs flying around in the background. The chairs and table were picked for their composition, as in the film hundreds of rods with their near to a thousand welds go flying around the room in a spectacular fashion.

As a boy, Platner liked to make birdhouses and sculptures. He studied at Cornell University, graduating in 1941 with a degree in architecture, and went on to work with Raymond Loewy, Eero Saarinen and I.M. Pei before opening his own practice. While so many of his compatriots were moulding plastics, Platner saw a gap in the market for something more glamorous. He "felt there was room for the kind of decorative, gentle, graceful kind of design that appeared in period style like Louis XV, but [with] a more rational base instead of being applied decoration." Questioning why the chair's support should be separate from its seat, he envisioned sitter, chair and stand as one. "I thought, why separate support from the object. Just make it all one thing. It starts at the floor and comes up and envelops me, supports me... What I wanted to achieve was a chair that, number one, was complementary to the person sitting in it, or to the person in the space between the wall and the chair." [103] Platner welded his curved, nickel-plated steel rods to circular frames which sculpturally served as structure and ornament on both the lounge and armchair, as the steel rods allowed the viewer to see the coloured padding from every angle of the chair, even when someone was sitting in it. Visually it looked like "a shiny sheath of wheat" according to Knoll International's catalogue at the time.

The Don Draper of interiors in the mid-sixties, Platner believed in designing from within and then moving outwards, rather than the other way around – and with this concept he bagged the most influential brands. He won great acclaim with his interiors for Ford Foundation headquarters, worked with Raymond Loewy, Eero Saarinen and Kevin Roche and is especially remembered for the interiors of JFK airport's iconic TWA terminal that he designed with Saarinen. He put Georg Jensen on the map with the Georg Jensen Design Center, using the kinds of glass partitions and projections only theatre designers had used up until then. Platner also won one of New York's top interior jobs of 1976, the glamorous Windows on the World restaurant which Paul Goldberger, then architecture critic of the *New York Times*, described as an example of "sensuous Modernism", with its lush interior, subdued pastels, fabric-covered walls and brass railings. But it is the wire collection of tables, chairs and sofa that really made his name among the public at large. The Platner Armchair has been in continuous production since its inception and, like the Cherner Armchair, has become a design Americans are justly proud of.

1966

Blow, Jonathan De Pas, Donato D'Urbino, Paolo Lomazzi and Carla Scolari, Zanotta SpA

Back in the days before bag recycling and concern over plastic, four young Italian architects came up with the perfect lounge chair for the laid back psychedelic generation. Designed in the Summer of Love using the principles of an inflatable raft, it harked back to the Michelin Man and Eileen Gray's Bibendum Chair of 1933 and was sold as an inexpensive piece in flat-pack form with the thoughtful addition of a puncture repair kit.

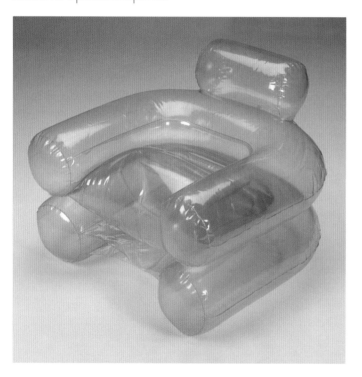

Flouting the older generation's bourgeois attachment to permanency, the four architects wanted to create a piece of furniture that was not intended to be kept for life and could not be passed down to the next generation. They pushed technology forward, calling for new advances in PVC welding that meant it could be bonded using high frequency waves without the need for stitching or a bonding fabric. It was essential that the piece was transparent as the architects wanted to fulfil Marcel Breuer's utopian dream of one day sitting on what Breuer called in 1925 "elastic columns of air".

After appearing in magazines the world over, the chair became a hit with the West's thrill-seeking mind-expanded youth. Because Blow could fold up small and was easy to export and store in shops it generated huge orders, making Zanotta an international name as a producer. This fun product would launch a plethora of pool furniture and toys, and secure a commission from Japan for a series of inflatable buildings that appeared at a Universal Expo in Osaka in 1970.

The architects went on to design a leather beanbag chair the same year as the Expo that mimicked a baseball glove and was called Joe after legendary baseball champion Joe DiMaggio.

1967

Seagull Chair, 3208, Arne Jacobsen, Fritz Hansen

While designing the Danish National Bank between the years 1965 and 1978 Arne Jacobsen conjured up a chair that would not only set off the strict lines of the building but also inspire passion in the interiors press. A progression on from the Series 7 chair, he cut deep into the silhouette of the Seagull Chair (3108) in 1969 and curving the laminated sliced veneer to fit into the curve in your back he gave hard-working bankers the comfort they needed while securing a heap of editorial praise for himself.

This highly sculpted, visually arresting chair was the talk of Copenhagen. People soon got word that some rather unusual looking chairs were featuring in their main bank. The teak version was used in the Danish National Bank's staff lunchroom while Seagulls with leather upholstery were created for both lounge and meeting rooms. Jacobsen installed Swan Chairs (page 146), with tables and sofas from his 3300 series, in the lobby and banking hall. He put his lamps in offices and corridors, and fitted doors with his famous door handle and bathrooms with those revolutionary Vola fittings that have been relentlessly copied around the world.

The last of his line of laminated stacking chairs, the Seagull was offered with carefully curved armrests and a slightly wider shell. Debuting as the 3208 at the Danish Furniture Fair in 1970, it proved a huge media success, and a small run of children's Seagulls were also made. But the extremely complicated moulding process saw twenty per cent of seats arrive off the production line with defects, and by the end of the seventies the chair was taken out of production as it no longer made commercial sense. Technology caught up in 2007 when a slightly larger Seagull was reintroduced and rechristened Lily.

93 Garden Egg Chair, Peter Ghyczy, Elastogran GmbH

Designed in West Germany and produced mainly in East Germany, a confusing trail of intrigue and deception makes the Garden Egg Chair by Peter Ghyczy all the more fascinating an object to own. Often highlighted as a typical example of sixties space age design, the portable polyurethane pod that opened to reveal a brightly coloured spongy fabric-covered seat and back was one of the earliest works by the Hungarian immigrant who was born on the Buda side of Budapest to aristocratic parents.

Ghyczy developed this portable outside chair, a kind of plastic suitcase you could sit in, to inspire his bosses and clients at the polyurethane factory Elastogran GmbH, where he was chief of design from 1968 to 1972. He wanted to show the limitless possibilities of the material but, after launching the initial prototype, production of the Garden Egg Chair was transferred to VEB Synthesewerk in Schwarzheide in 1970, an East German company who bought manufacturing technology from Elastogran.

Unbeknown to Ghyczy, who was told the chair was far too expensive for his West German factory to produce, VEB Synthesewerk was contractually obliged to manufacture 15,000 pieces of polyurethane furniture as part payment for the Elastogran machines they had bought, including a substantial number of Garden Egg Chairs. Chemist and owner Gottfried Reuter had landed in financial difficulties and was involved in a variety of scandals that culminated in his rather mysterious death in a hotel room in East Berlin in 1986.

When Jana Scholze, curator of Modern Furniture and Product Design at London's Victoria & Albert Museum, interviewed the production manager at the East German factory in 2010, she was surprised he had not been allowed any contact with Ghyczy, even when the design had to be slightly altered. He and his workers were proud to be associated with such an extraordinary piece from the West and he would have loved to have met or at least spoken to the designer.

"Since he did not get any royalties he thought that the chair was not selling," says Ghyczy's son Felix, who grew up with his father's most recognized design in the garden of their house in Holland. Ghyczy was always designing and money was not his prime motivator so he worked in a bit of a bubble. "Our home was full of my father's designs, old and new. But when in 1998 I did a study on the Garden Egg to see if a reintroduction would be possible he was very surprised at how desirable and copied the chair had become." [104]

While Ghyczy went on to invent a revolutionary frameless glass dining table in 1970, Elastogran GmbH went bankrupt in 1973, with production continuing solely for the East European market until it was halted in 1975 after around 14,000 Garden Egg Chairs had been made. Vintage productions will therefore have either the Lemförde mark and a line saying something like "In Ordnung, Abt. Qk, 9. Juni 1971", a sign they were one of the very few made in Lemförde, West Germany, or a Schwarzheide mark, which would suggest they were made in East Germany with no royalties given to Ghyczy, who never sold the rights. Without either of these you are probably looking at a Chinese copy, according to Ghyczy's son. If you are unable to find a West German original, head to Ghyczy Selection BV, based in the Netherlands, where Felix and his father still manufacture the chair in a limited number and every piece is numbered and signed by the master himself.

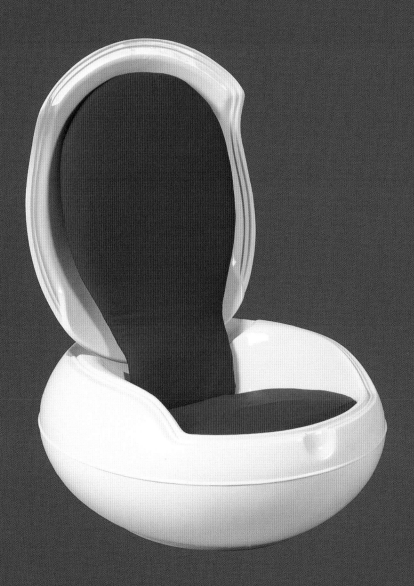

1968

94 Soft Pad Chair, 217, Charles and Ray Eames, Herman Miller

Charles and Ray worked for longer and harder than most of their contemporaries so it is not surprising that they managed to produce the office chair that midcentury collectors swear by for comfort. The Soft Pad evolved from the Aluminium Group which was originally designed for the American industrialist J. Irwin Miller who needed a good outdoor chair to sit visiting dignitaries in after he commissioned Eero Saarinen to design him a house in Indiana.

The Eameses went a step further and created a multi-tasking chair (with Alexander Girard consulting on fabrics) that could be used inside and outside as well as around a table. A masterful piece of engineering, the 1958 cast aluminium chair has a seat frame with a continuous piece of synthetic mesh stretched between its ergonomically curved aluminium ribs. Its comfort pocket, inspired by hammocks and camp chairs made the chairs lighter and more comfortable than the traditional upholstered wooden or metal-backed office chairs available at the time. The curve on the strengthening horizontal metal rib sits away from the body at the back and doubles as a handle which allows you to pull the office chair inside or outside, or from your desk to a meeting room or a collaborator's workspace.

Eames Soft Pads in their low (217) and high-backed (219) incarnations sat somewhere between the aforementioned Aluminium Group and the Lobby Chair (page 154) in terms

of design. The one pictured here is the chair I sit on in my own workspace, an early version sourced from America, with a tilting mechanism created by the simple act of screwing and unscrewing a bolt underneath. It has a twisting system in the central stand just above the four legs that moves the chair slightly up and down.

New versions come with the same tilt mechanism, but with an improved lift and drop, and now have five legs on castors, or four without. The leather on more recent productions does not have such a wonderful sumptuous feel, brought about by years of sitting on this sturdy piece, but the tweaks made over the years have made it easier to adjust.

The Eameses were always willing to learn, allowing materials to dictate and designs to evolve in front of them. In one early archive image where Charles is seen photographing a Soft Pad upholstered in wool with a lifted pin-tucked edge, you see the pillows of the design sagging a little. Even though customers occasionally ordered or reupholstered Soft Pads in their own fabric, the intended final designs were in leather, plumper thanks to extra foam filling and made more durable with a flattened double-stitched edge. This type of stitch took twice as long to achieve, using two different sewing machines. It has stood the test of time in my 1969 production and in early Fehlbaum 'Herman Miller International' Eames Soft Pad chairs which have the same well worn and comfortable fit as a vintage Herman Miller.

1969

95 UP5 Donna, Gaetano Pesce, C&B Italia

Remember the fight scene in *Diamonds Are Forever* where a henchwoman in hot pants called Bambi and her bikini clad associate Thumper battle it out with Bond between Pierre Paulin's Ribbon Chair and Gaetano Pesce's Donna in the living room of John Lautner's Elrod House in Palm Springs? Or those Magnum images of Sean Connery seen relaxing between takes with his head nestled between the chair's "breasts"? You wonder whether the man who played one of movie history's most celebrated womanizers knew that Pesce's anthropomorphic chair was a clarion call to the world at large to take women's rights seriously, or that its abstract female shape and elastic-linked ball as footstool (UP6) symbolized the ball and chain of women's subjugation. Dressed in bold colours or a Bridget Riley stripe, Pesce's Donna celebrated a more liberated woman as psychedelia and women's lib started to inspire fashion and interiors.

The Italian designer and architect was originally looking to make a sofa cast from a car when he happened upon a machine used for building insulation that sprayed polyurethane foam in between the gaps in walls. He started playing around with it and it gave him an idea. Taking the regrowth of squashed "cells" in a squeezed sponge as inspiration, Pesce oversaw the development of a new type of polyurethane with a different chemical formula that would allow him to squeeze his chairs down to a portable size. So, once the moulded blocks of foam had been covered in nylon jersey and packaged in a special PVC invented for the purpose, they were decreased to ten per cent of their size in a vacuum chamber, perfect for retail storage and delivery from warehouse to store. Described by Pesce as "transformation furniture", [105] UP5 was intended to make the owner feel very much a part of the design process – they would open a flat-pack and see their Donna, or any other of the UP pieces, grow majestically in front of them.

> **"If you have something to say that is important, your opinion about a political event, etcetera, then through the object you express that. Your opinion goes immediately to a lot of people, and that is why design is important."** [106]
>
> Gaetano Pesce

The chair's metamorphosis was not as instant as Pesce hoped – it took about an hour – and the design was not without its problems. Over time the lack of air made the foam deteriorate in the packaging, which was a terrible setback for Pesce as buyers lost confidence. You can now buy a non-inflatable version of the chair, relaunched by the manufacturer, renamed B&B Italia, for the millennium. A child's version was released in 2014.

1969

96 Birillo Bar Stool, Joe Colombo, Zanotta

Around the time the first man landed on the moon, Joe Colombo was on his own mission: to reinvent interiors. With a background in industrial design and his father's electrical conductor factory as his playground, he honed his craft until he could open his own studio and set about creating futuristic habitats like the ones he produced for the second Visiona – the famous yearly design installation sponsored by chemicals company Bayer AG on board a ship docked in Cologne between 1968 and 1974. His Total Furnishing Unit of 1971 featured an integrated television in the ceiling and swivelling walls with integrated minibars. Night Cell was a sleeping pod designed to close and switch to climate control in Barbarella-style fashion, while Kitchen-Box was a dynamic modular kitchen-diner that you could move around a room, featuring a pull-out dining table and air conditioning.

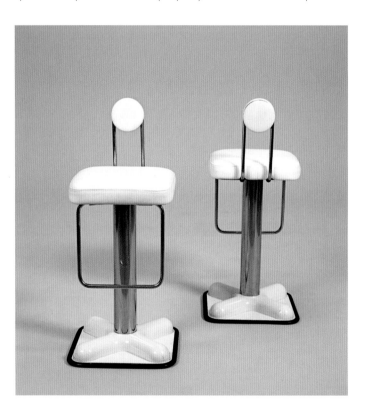

By the time Colombo designed the Birillo (which literally translates as bar stool) he had won a handful of medals at Milan's Triennale, with three of his pieces already on exhibition in the permanent collection at MOMA. The revolving bar stools were just part of a series that included a bistro table and armchair intended for bars, restaurants and clubs. The chrome-plated tubular steel framework with its vinyl covered steel-plate seat and the most minimal of backrests dotted into a metal clip at the back has a space age meets Bauhaus look. The moulded ABS plastic foot glides on four castors, like a spaceship making ready to land.

Although arguably not as popular to collect as the Boby Trolley storage unit, Elda Armchair (page 165) and Universale (page 178), the race is on to nab these when they pop up at our midcentury modern shows. Birillo was one of the last things Colombo designed before he died unexpectedly from a heart attack at the age of forty-one. It was 30 July 1971, the same day he was born.

1970-1

The OMK stacking chair, or Omkstak, bounced into Habitat stores with childish verve in a choice of red, green, yellow, black and white dressed with a lick of epoxy resin. This new star of a chair, with its industrially spray-painted and perforated pressed-steel seat, and its short back that clipped, screwed and tucked into a continuous tubular steel frame, packed quite a punch when first released in 1971. Fresh out of the prestigious Central School of Art (now Central Saint Martins) in London, with a thirst for early Modernism and the Bauhaus and a passion for tubular steel, Rodney Kinsman and Polish designer Jurek Olejnik set up OMK Design with British band manager Bryan Morrison in 1965, using initials from their surnames. Terence Conran snapped up their early designs and, after a few years of designing furniture aimed at thrifty homeowners for what was then an embryonic Habitat chain, they looked more towards the contract market.

What looks like inspiration from the Swiss Landi (page 32) and a lesson in stacking from David Rowland's 40/4 (page 174) "was actually inspired by the automotive industry and more specifically the Willy's Jeep" according to Kinsman. "The monocoque seat panel is reminiscent of the jeep bonnet, and forms the main structural element of the chair, eliminating the need for crossrails. The punched holes in the seat and back are not purely aesthetic; they reduce weight and the flanged holes strengthen the sheet." [107] Fun, cheap and indestructible, these mass-produced chairs could stack up to twenty-five high, and had a handle at the top for ease of movement. You can now get a galvanized version, although original OMKs are designed for use inside and outside. The license

was taken on by Bieffe, the Italian producers of Joe Colombo's Boby Trolley, for whom Kinsman designed a range of products during the seventies and eighties including the Tokyo Stool and Orbit Mirror. The Omkstak pressed-steel stacking chair proved a huge success worldwide, with British designer Kinsman going on to design many more award-winning public seating systems.

98 Synthesis 45 Typist Chair, Z9/r, Ettore Sottsass Jr, Olivetti

Austrian-born Italian designer Ettore Sottsass Jr was not just about play, as everyone likes to make out. He was both humorous and serious, and hated it when people called him a Futurist, says Barbara Radice, the author and journalist who became his wife. "Ettore used to say that he was not interested in the future, only in the present." [108]

Originally trained as an architect like his father before him, Sottsass Jr escaped from a Yugoslavian concentration camp in his twenties after being told every day was the last day of his life. A natural survivor, he could put his hand to anything and worked by the philosophy that daily life and objects could be made more appealing for people. A keen photographer, philosopher, designer, painter, ceramicist and friend of the Beat poets, his big break came when he was hired to work at Olivetti alongside Adriano Olivetti's son, Roberto, and the engineer Mario Tchou after a stint with George Nelson in New York in the fifties. Given free rein with a studio and his own design assistants and engineers, Sottsass helped Olivetti design Italy's first mainframe computer and won the Golden Compass for a calculator in 1970.

Sottsass soon turned his focus to the office interior which, at that time in Italy, was overrun with heavy and expensive furniture. He wanted to make the office more sensual and exciting, and also make it function more efficiently. Like the much-coveted lipstick red typewriter that he launched with Olivetti on Valentine's Day in 1970, his Synthesis 45 series of 1971–3 appealed to the new, cool office crowd. Dubbed "45" as a reference to the 45-centimetre base measurements used, the series was fun, cheap and mass-produced, and covered everything from an office that folded out of a cupboard to modular accessories designed to hold pens, papers, paperclips, phones, typewriters and calculating equipment. Furniture could be chopped and changed and adapted for different workers' needs, side tables and drawers could be swapped from left to right, and paper trays raised to the right height for each worker and moved around on swivel joints. Sottsass saw a vision of computers incorporated into home and office and Synthesis desks were already designed to accommodate them when his prophecy came true.

Office managers were keen to have the Z9/r chair with its space-age base that swivelled on a moving central pole. Designed to move from telephone to computer to filing cabinet in a flash, the chair could spin across a room on its wheels and took up very little space. Its injection-moulded ABS frame was long lasting, the textile-covered foam seat comfortable, and a mixed palette of colours helped office managers match furniture with the mood or branding of the office.

Terence Conran loved the range so much that, once established as sole agent in the UK, he gave the Z9/r chair its own advertisement. Once customers had fallen for the chair they often bought other parts of the Synthesis series to match. One of the first designers to tap into the way people attach emotion to even the most practical objects, Sottsass Jr's philosophy was one that designer Jonathan Ive would later use to Apple's advantage. But rather than pursuing the big money in office design, Sottsass Jr sped off in another direction, like his typist's chair, founding the radical Memphis group at an age when most designers would choose retirement over a new experimental direction.

"To me design... is a way of discussing society, politics, eroticism, food and even design." [109]

Ettore Sottsass Jr

1971

99 Falcon Chair, Sigurd Resell, Vatne Lenestolfabrikk

When designer Sigurd Resell's Falcon Chair first rolled off the production line and into the shops, Norway had never seen sales quite like it. Scandinavia's answer to the Chair, with its luxurious plump leather cushions lining a canvas sling-seat hooked to a metal frame and hovering over a chrome splay base, was the first chair buyers put in their shop windows. Knut and Ivar Saeter had worried that their bigger, brighter factory in Vatne might not be able to sustain itself as orders had been slow in the two years since it was built in 1969. But once Resell was installed as a designer everything changed. Norwegians were quick to take his extraordinary looking Falcon Chair into their hearts and sales at Vatne spiralled.

Sigurd Resell kicked off his career after Niels Vodder, the Danish master carpenter behind many of Finn Juhl's finest pieces, praised one of the young designer's drawings in a competition. A prototype of what would become the SR600 was made from the drawing a few years later and, in 1958, the chair won an award at the Copenhagen Cabinetmakers' Guild Exhibition.

Resell's Falcon Chairs were most commonly sold as a pair, and often with a matching glass and chrome and steel legged table. There was also a low, rectangular wood-topped coffee table with chrome and steel legs, but when both high and low-backed models proved too expensive for export because of their metal frames, the steel was exchanged for lightweight laminated wood, causing yet another spike in sales from 1974. Kåre Naustdal, who sold Vatne furniture in the United States through Norvud, said that it would not be unusual in the course of a morning to receive a handful of orders for Falcons by the container-load from his American clients.

The chair's popularity led to it being copied around the world. Vatne took one Danish manufacturer to court – they had a version of the design with the name Superstar. Vatne won.

1971

100 Wiggle Side Chair, Frank Gehry, Easy Edges

In 1964 a British designer called Peter Murdoch created a chair from a single piece of die-cut, folded polyurethane card. Designed to be disposable, it was the perfect piece of Pop furniture. Architect Frank Gehry's longer-lasting Wiggle Side Chair materialized eight years later. Gehry wanted to create something softer than the plastic pieces he was seeing emerge around him, like the corduroys hippies had started wearing around his home town of Los Angeles. Lovingly carved from a redundant pile of corrugated cardboard he used for building architecture models, Gehry gave the collection of sculpted furniture the name Easy Edges after the edge board from which it was made.

Gehry's work is very much a product of his upbringing in Los Angeles – a magical, experimental, ever-changing place where he saw Richard Neutra and Rudolph Schindler make their mark at the beginning of the midcentury movement in architecture. But his Wiggle Side Chair also suggests a knowledge of the work of Alvar Aalto, the way he used the curve in his furniture to strengthen his pieces, and of Panton and his all-in-one plastic chair.

His father, an art-loving boxer and salesman, introduced him to paper as a child, when they fashioned hobby horses out of papier mâché. And Gehry returned to making sculptures in quieter moments at his architectural practice. For Wiggle he set about cutting and gluing sixty layers of corrugated edge board in alternating directions, secured with hidden screws and clamped each side with hardboard. Wiggle looked like a snake about to unfold and slither around the room. The folds made it sturdy, the fabric ensured it felt warm to sit on and the texture of the cardboard had an incredible noise-reducing effect in a room.

Gehry thought it would be a bit of fun and extra cash, but once the architectural chairs had made a splash in the design world, demand was overwhelming. The line made it into Bloomingdale's with a family of other pieces, surrounded by a system of cardboard walls and floors, but orders flooded in and the studio became chaotic. In March 1990 Gehry professed at a TED talk, "It threw me through a loop. I wasn't secure enough as an architect." Not wanting to turn his space into the next Eames Office, Gehry stopped production of Easy Edges. "I started to feel threatened. I closed myself off for weeks at a time in a room to rethink my life. I decided that I was an architect, not a furniture designer... I simply stopped doing it."[110]

Experimental Edges followed, a collection of items that have since become museum pieces, made to be intentionally bizarre and impractical so that Gehry would not have to mass produce them. As his architecture became more well known and people started to snap up every cardboard piece Gehry had ever produced, Vitra took on Easy Edges and started producing four models from the collection in 1986, including Wiggle Side Chair, Side Chair and Low Table Set. Today, the earliest pieces are highly sought after and the Easy Edges series is still in production.

And so we end our book with memories of early masters who stripped chairs back to the bare essentials, creating miraculous curves or startling geometry using anything at their disposal. But it is not enough to simply focus on designers who deconstruct and reinvent. If the midcentury movement has taught us anything it is this: knowing the story of the commitment and passion behind each piece makes us more considerate consumers when it comes to what we invest in.

1972

About the author

Lucy Ryder Richardson
Daughter of a vintage car enthusiast and lover of all things Scandinavian, writer Lucy Ryder Richardson was a successful fashion journalist writing for publications including Vogue and the Guardian before she moved to a sixties house in a wood in Dulwich on the outskirts of London and set up a showhome with business partner Petra Curtis in 2003. They held open houses that mixed midcentury and modern to wide acclaim in her home which led to larger shows held at various buildings known for their midcentury and Brutalist architecture and pop-ups of favourites from the Modern Marketplace including London's top design show Design Junction. Now co-owner of the hugely successful brand Modern Shows Lucy has not only written this book, but also helps run and market the shows, forges partnerships with brands including Elle Decoration, writes for both blogs Inside Modernism and Destination Modernism and runs her own midcentury location house. www.modernshows.com

Author's Thanks
I must say a huge thank you to Kevin Dutton for the incredible photos he takes and digitally manipulates at every Haggerston show including the Warren Platner chair that turned out to be a rather good fake after he had taken hours to painstakingly fill in the background between every spindle (I haven't told him yet) and to Christie's and Jacksons and all the families and PRs who loaned their images without expecting any payment in return. Thank you to my wonderful Mum and Dad for coming to my shows and telling me how proud they are with tears in their eyes even though they don't particularly like midcentury furniture. Thank you to Molly and Bert who had to put up with a tableful of books and papers and the occasional grouch from 'Mum'. To Pavilion's lovely Katie Cowan who has been waiting to do something with Modern Shows since she first came to our shows ten years ago and the equally delightful Amy Christian who held my hand the whole way through. But the most special pair of thank yous go to Petra Curtis and Tanya Pateman for giving me the time to write the book while they soldiered on at Modern Shows. Can I write another book please?

Publisher's Thanks
Thank you to Emily Asquith for her amazing attention to detail while copyediting, and thanks to Emily Hedges for meticulous record keeping and picture research. Thanks also to Zoë Anspach and Gemma Wilson for their work on the book design.

Contributors

Petra Curtis This former graphic designer who co-founded Modern Shows with Lucy compiled our indispensable directory of recommended dealers. Petra Curtis shares her father's verve for organization; he managed the Pasadena Roof Orchestra for more than a decade. Constantly expanding the Modern Marketplace as well as finding bigger and better experts in all areas of C20 collectables for the shows Petra has a keen eye for the kinds of locations Modern Shows' visitors will love including London's Brutalist gem, the Erno Goldfinger building in Haggerston. Petra's latest projects include sourcing for Brindisa restaurants and properties around London, a facet of the business the duo are keen to expand. Lucy and business partner Petra are often called upon for quotes on mid-C20 collectables. The duo now hold six shows a year around London and are looking to franchise to midcentury and marketing experts in other cities around the world. **www.themodernmarketplace.com**

Kevin Dutton Son of an Ole Wanscher enthusiast, this photographer for over twenty years has a passion for midcentury design and architectural plants. Kevin kickstarted his career taking photos of artists, musicians and performers for newspapers and magazines in the mid nineties. Since then, he has worked in the UK and abroad for a wide variety of editorial, design and business clients. He now works in collaboration with various creatives producing images of furniture, interiors, architecture, fashion and textiles, ceramics, sculpture and fine art. Kevin's stunning, high resolution images are now sold as fine art photographic prints at art fairs and galleries. Apple Inc loved his purple Allium shot on black so much they bought it for their wallpaper. **www.kevindutton.net**

Jacksons Thank you to Paul and Carina Jackson for providing so many of the photographs for this book. Since opening their first gallery in the heart of Stockholm in 1981, this British Swedish duo has formed an important collection of Scandinavian and international design covering all disciplines of the twentieth century. In 2008, Jacksons launched a satellite space in "das Galerienhaus" in Berlin that provides collectors and museums with the opportunity to view specially curated exhibitions while enjoying the numerous galleries in the art district of Kreuzberg/Mitte. The gallery promotes the work of a number of midcentury designers working in furniture, lighting, ceramics, glass and textiles with highlights include Poul Kjaerholm, Alvar and Aino Aalto, Nanna Ditzel, Josef Frank, Grete Jalk, Finn Juhl, Kaare Klint, Bruno Mathsson and Hans J. Wegner. **www.jacksons.se**

Christie's Thank you to Simon Andrews, Modern Design Specialist at Christie's London, and his team for raking through their archives in order to fill in some of our visual gaps. Christie's, the world's oldest fine art auctioneer, offers around 450 auctions annually in over 80 categories, including all areas of fine and decorative arts, jewellery, photographs, collectibles, wine and more and has a long

and successful history conducting private sales for its clients in all categories, with emphasis on Post-War & Contemporary, Impressionist & Modern and Old Masters and Jewellery. With 54 offices in 32 countries and 12 salerooms around the world including London, New York, Paris, Geneva, Milan, Amsterdam, Dubai, Zürich, Hong Kong, Shanghai and Mumbai, Christie's has more recently led the market with expanded initiatives in Russia, China, India and the United Arab Emirates and successful sales and exhibitions in Beijing, Mumbai and Dubai.
www.christies.com

Special thanks go to designers or their partners, children and grandchildren as well as the family and friends of the producers for their help with this book and especially to: Benjamin Cherner, Marianne Wegner, Felix Ghyczy, Paula Day, Celia Bertoia, Dennie Ditzel, Federica Zanuso, Rodney Kinsman, Henriette Coray, Benjamin Paulin, Barbara Radice, Brita-Lena Ekström, Yoichi Nakamuta, Mogens S. Koch, Tami Komai, Marianne Panton, Mira Nakashima, Martine Eskes, Wim Rietveld, Hans Benthe Mathiesen, Thomas Graversen, Hans Henrik Sørensen, Ole Jørgensen, Tobias Jacobsen, Henrik Lund Larsen, Daniel Ostroff and Eames Demetrios.

Thanks also to the Press and Archive at: MOMA, Alvar Aalto Museum, Artek, Noguchi Museum, Vitra, Skandium, Herman Miller, Knoll, Carl Hansen & Son, Adelta, Noguchi Foundation, Cassina, B&B Italia, Zanotta, One Collection, PP Møbler, The Cale Schiang Partnership, Ercol, Fredericia, Fritz Kramer, Zanuso, Swedese, Pictoright, Race Furniture, Ahrend, Camron PR, Fjord Fiesta, Artifort, Colombo Archives, Spectrum Design, OMK Design, Eames Office and Frank Gehry's Foga.

For the cover illustration, thanks goes to Hyperkit, a London-based graphic design studio founded by Tim Balaam and Kate Sclater. Their long-standing collaboration with Lucy and Petra of Modern Shows has led to the creation of a strong and recognisable identity for their events which uses silhouette illustrations of chairs and other items typically on display.
www.hyperkit.co.uk

Picture credits

The publisher would like to thank the following sources for their kind permission to reproduce the photographs in this book. Every effort has been made to clear the necessary rights, but any amendments or omissions can be corrected in future editions.

Ch = © Christie's Images Limited (2016); J = © Jacksons SE; MS = © Modern Shows, photographer Kevin Dutton

Cover illustration and page 1 © Hyperkit; page 5 J; 7 © DACS 2016, photo J; 11 Ch; 13 MS; 15 Carl Hansen & Søn; 16 J; 17 Cassina Spa, photo J; 19 J; 21 Tolix ®, photo MS; 23 Cassina Spa, photo Ch; 25 © ADAGP, Paris and DACS, London 2016, photo Ch; 27 courtesy of Isokon Plus (www.isokonplus.com), photo J; 29 J; 31 MS; 33 MS; 35 J; 37 © ADAGP, Paris and DACS, London 2016, photo Pernette Perriand-Barsac. Archives Charlotte Perriand; 39 and 41 © ONECOLLECTION; 43 courtesy of Knoll, Inc.; 44 and 45 courtesy of George Nakashima Woodworkers; 47 MS; 49 MS; 50 © ONECOLLECTION; 51 J; 53 MS; 54 MS; 57 MS; 59 Ch; 60 Fritz Hansen; 61 MS; 62 © PP Mobler; 63 J; 64 Carl Hansen & Søn/Luis Valdizon; 65 Ch; 67 Dunbar Furniture, photo © Christie's Images Limited; 69 MS; 70 MS; 71 Peter Stackpole/Getty Images; 72 © Carl Hansen & Søn; 73 Cassina Spa; 75 Ch; 76 © ONECOLLECTION; 79 MS; 80 CBS Photo Archive/Getty Images; 82 J; 83 J; 85 MS; 86 Carl Hansen & Søn; 87 DIGITAL IMAGE © 2016, The Museum of Modern Art/Scala, Florence; 88 and 89 J; 90 © The Robin and Lucienne Day Foundation; 91 MS; 93 MS; 95 Ch; 96 Fritz Hansen; 99 Cassina Spa; 101 MS; 102 Fritz Hansen; 105 photograph by Joshua McHugh. Courtesy of Knoll, Inc.; 106 from the Knoll Archive. Courtesy of Knoll, Inc.; 107 Advertisement for Bertoia Diamond Chairs, designed by Herbert Matter. Knoll Archive. Courtesy of Knoll, Inc; 108 Ch; 109 MS; 111 Ch; 113 MS; 115 MS; 117 J; 118 © The Isamu Noguchi Foundation and Garden Museum/ARS, New York and DACS, London, photo Ch; 119 courtesy of Zanotta Spa – Italy, photo © Zanotta Archives; 120 courtesy of Herman Miller, Inc., photo MS; 123 © V&A Images/Alamy Stock Photo; 125 John Bryson/Getty Images; 127 MS; 129 MS; 131 MS; 133 courtesy of Herman Miller, Inc.; 134 courtesy of Herman Miller, Inc., photo MS; 135 © Arcaid Images/Alamy Stock Photo; 137 J; 138 MS; 139 MS; 141 © ADAGP, Paris and DACS, London 2016, photo MS; 142 Cassina Spa, photo J; 143 MS; 144 Frances Chandler; 145 courtesy of Cherner Chair Co., photo MS; 147 MS; 148 Fritz Hansen; 149 Design: Verner Panton, © Vitra (www.vitra.com) photographer Marc Eggimann; 150 © Keld Helmer-Petersen; 151 Skovdal & Skovdal; 152 J; 153 MS; 155 MS; 157 Artifort; 159 Design: Verner Panton, © Vitra (www.vitra.com) photographer Hans Hansen; 160 Verner Panton Design; 162 MS; 163 G Plan; 164 Skandium (www.skandium.com); 165 J; 167 J; 168 © AF archive/Alamy Stock Photo; 169 J; 171 Aarnio Design Ltd, Harri Kosonen, Studio Sempre; 173 courtesy of Knoll, Inc.; 175 courtesy of Herman Miller, Inc.; 176 Artifort; 177 MS; 178 Ignazia Favata/Studio Joe Colombo; 179 © Béton Brut; 181 photography by Ilan Rubin, courtesy of Knoll, Inc.; 182 courtesy of Zanotta Spa – Italy, photo J; 183 J; 185 MS, 187 MS; 189 B&B Italia (bebitalia.com); 190 J; 191 Omstak; 193 © ADAGP, Paris and DACS, London 2016, photo: Jean-Pierre Maurer; 194 MS; 197 Ch.

UNITED KINGDOM

1934 — www.abelsloane1934.com
20th Century Furnishing —
　　www.20thcenturyfurnishing.co.uk
20th Century Marks — www.20thcenturymarks.co.uk
20thcquarters — www.20thcquarters.com
Alto Stile — www.altostile.com
Apollo — www.apolloantiques.com
August Interiors — www.augustinteriors.co.uk
BB Bespoke — www.bbbespoke.co.uk
Beldi Rugs — www.beldirugs.com
BETON BRUT — www.betonbrut.co.uk
C20 Home — www.c20home.co.uk
C20C — www.c20c.com
Chase & Sorensen — www.chaseandsorensen.com
Cream and Chrome — www.creamandchrome.co.uk
Dagmar — www.dagmar-london.com
Danish Homestore — www.danish-homestore.com
De Parma — www.deparma.com
Decorative Modern — www.decorativemodern.co.uk
Designs of Modernity — www.designsofmodernity.com
Diagonal Furniture — www.diagonalfurniture.com
Elemental — www.elemental.uk.com
Elephant and Monkey — www.elephantandmonkey.co.uk
Elliott and Tate — www.elliottandtate.com
Fandango Interiors — www.fandangointeriors.co.uk
Flure Grossart — www.fluregrossart.com
Fragile — www.fragiledesign.com
GP Light and More — www.gplightandmore.com
Hayloft Mid-century — www.midcenturyhome.co.uk
House of Twenty — www.houseoftwenty.com
Johanna Pinder-Wilson —
　　www.johannapinder-wilson.com
Johnny Moustache — www.johnnymoustache.com
L & V Art and Design — www.landvdesign.com
Lovely & Co — www.lovelyandco.co.uk
MAR-DEN — www.mar-den.co.uk
MCM Interiors — www.mcm-interiors.co.uk
Metroretro — www.metroretro.co.uk
Midmode — www.midmode.co.uk
Modern Antique — www.modernantique.net
Modern Room — www.modernroom.co.uk
Muir — www.tetburyantiques.com
Nanadobbie — www.nanadobbie.com
norepro — www.norepro.co.uk
Object d'epoch — www.objectdepoch.com
Pelikan — www.pelikanonline.co.uk
Philip Varma — www.philipvarma.com
Pink Flamingos — www.pink-flamingos.co.uk
Pure Imagination — www.pureimaginations.co.uk
Retro Bazaar — www.retro-bazaar.co.uk
Retro Living — www.retroliving.co.uk
Retrouvius — www.retrouvius.com
Rocket Gallery — www.jensrisom.com
Sarah Potter — www.sarahpotter.co.uk

Scandi-Mod — www.scandi-mod.com
Scandinavian by Design — www.sbydonline.com
Scott Campbell — www.scottcampbellmodern.blogspot.com
Sweet Vintage — www.sweet-vintage.com
The Furniture Rooms — www.thefurniturerooms.co.uk
The Gifted Few — www.thegiftedfew.com
The Modern Marketplace —
　　www.themodernmarketplace.com
The Modern Warehouse —
　　www.themodernwarehouse.com
Twentieth Century Antiques —
　　www.twentiethcenturyantiques.co.uk
twentytwentyone — www.twentytwentyone.com/vintage
Vintage Unit — www.vintageunit.com
WEMM — www.wemm.co.uk
Whittaker Gray — www.whittakergray.co.uk

AUSTRALIA

Angelucci 20th Century — www.angelucci.net.au
Cabinet de Luxe — www.cabinetdeluxe.com.au
Danish Red — www.danishred.com.au
Grandfathers Axe — www.grandfathersaxe.com.au
Modern Times — www.moderntimes.com.au
Our Space Interiors — www.ourspaceinteriors.com
Retro on Regent — www.retroonregent.com.au
Virtanen Antiques — www.virtanen-antiques.com

AUSTRIA

Design and Art — www.designandart.at
Galerie Zeitloos — www.zeitloos.at
Lichterloh — www.lichterloh.com
MADERO Collectors Room — www.madero.at
Michaela Bauer — www.michaelabauer.com
Rauminhalt — www.rauminhalt.at
The Room — www.theroom.uk.com
Tony Subal Gallery — www.tonysubal.com
Vampt Vintage Design — www.vamptvintagedesign.com
Vintagerie — www.vintagerie.at

BELGIUM

1000 Designs — www.1000designs.be
20eme Siecle — www.20emesiecle.be
20th Century Deco-Arts — www.deco-arts.be
46 Kloosterstraat — www.46kloosterstraat.com
Ampersand House — www.ampersandhouse.com
Apostrophe — www.apostrophe1.com
Axel Pairon — www.axelpairon.com
City-furniture — www.city-furniture.be
Dierbaar Design — www.dierbaardesign.com
Fins de Siècles et Plus Gallery — www.fins-de-siecles.be
Funky Vintage — www.funkyvintage.be
furniture-love.com — www.furniture-love.com
Galerie 2010 — www.galerie-2010.be
Galerie Le Beau — www.galerie-lebeau.com
Gallery Gush — www.gallerygush.com

Gallery Vanlandschoote — www.vanlandschoote.com
Goldwood by Boris — www.goldwoodbyboris.com
Haute Antiques Gallery — www.hauteantiques207.be
Jimmy Beyens — www.jimmybeyens.com
Made in Denmark — www.madeindenmark.be
Møbelfabrik — www.mobelfabrik.be
Modest Furniture — www.modestfurniture.com
More Than a House — www.morethanahouse.be
Olivier Biltereyst — www.olibil.com
Pellegrini Design — www.pellegrinidesign.be
Polyedre — www.polyedre.be
Thomas Serruys — www.thomasserruys.com
Vintage Design Point — www.vintage-design-point.be

CANADA

By Design Modern — www.bydesignmodern.com
Full House Modern — www.fullhouseconsign.com
MCM Refinishing — www.mcmrefinishing.com
Mostly Danish — www.mostlydanishfurniture.ca
Porch Modern — www.porchmodern.com
Scandinavian.Modern — www.scandinavianmod.com
The Fabulous Find — www.thefabulousfind.ca

CZECH REPUBLIC

Czech Avant Garde — www.czechavantgarde.com
DEBYT — www.debyt.cz
funkcionalista — www.funkcionalista.cz

DENMARK

A Petersen Collection & Craft — www.apetersen.dk
CC Danish Modern — www.cc-danish-modern.com
Kemnitz — www.kemnitz.dk
Dansk Møbelkunst — www.dmk.dk
Gallery Wernberg — www.gallerywernberg.com
House of Design — www.houseofdesign.dk
klassik — www.klassik.dk
Osted Antik — www.osted-antik.dk
reModern.dk — www.remodern.dk
Roxy Klassik — www.roxyklassik.dk
Secher Fine Art & Design — www.secherfineart.com
Svendborg Antikvitets & Kunsthandel —
　　www.antikogdesign.dk
The Apartment — www.theapartment.dk

FINLAND

art.fi — www.art.fi
Design Dealers Finland — www.designdealers.fi
Gallerie Linna — www.gallerielinna.com
Helsinki Secondhand — www.helsinkisecondhand.fi
Stool — www.stool.fi

FRANCE

2021design — www.2021design.com
Brice Bérard — www.briceberard.com
Collection of Design — www.collectionofdesign.fr

Cornershop Design — www.cornershop-design.com
Déjà Vu — www.design-dejavu.com
Eric Philippe — www.ericphilippe.com
Espace Camille — www.espacecamille.com
Fiftease — www.fiftease.com
Franck Laigneau — www.francklaigneau.com
Galerie 44 — www.galerie44.com
Galerie 54 — www.galerie54.com
Galerie Downtown — www.galeriedowntown.com
Galerie Jacques Lacoste — www.jacqueslacoste.fr
Galerie Kreo — www.galeriekreo.com
Galerie Møbler — www.galerie-mobler.com
Galerie Pascal Cuisinier — www.galeriepascalcuisinier.com
Galerie Patrick Seguin — www.patrickseguin.com
Intérieurs Modernes — www.interieursmodernes.fr
Jousse Entreprise — www.jousse-entreprise.com
Mandalian Paillard — www.mandalianpaillard.com
Meubles et Lumières — www.meublesetlumieres.com
Modernariato — www.modernariato.fr
Tack — www.tack-market.com
Twig7 — www.twig7.fr

GERMANY
19 West Furniture — www.19west.de
breuerhouse — www.breuerhouse.com
Coroto — www.coroto.de
Design Scout — www.design-scout.net
Firma London — www.firmalondon.com
formformsuche — www.formformsuche.de
galerie fifty fifty — www.galerie-fiftyfifty.de
Galerie für Architektenmöbel —
        www.architektenmoebelgalerie.de
inside-room — www.inside-room.de
Interior Aksel — www.interior-aksel.de
Jochum Rodgers — www.jochumrodgers.de
Frank Landau — www.franklandau.com
frankfurt-minimal — www.frankfurt-minimal.de
Klassik — www.klassik.dk
Kunzenhof20 — www.kunzenhof20.de
Matkoline — www.matkoline.com
mid century design — www.midcenturydesign.de
minimalconcept.de — www.minimalconcept.de
Original in Berlin — www.originalinberlin.com
Politura — www.politura-berlin.de
René Berlin — www.rene.berlin
ROOM OF ART — www.room-of-art.de
Schoen Design — www.schoendesign.org

IRELAND
Kirk Modern — www.kirkmodern.com
Midcentury On Line — www.mid-centuryonline.com

ITALY
âgé — www.agemodernariato.com
Antiquariando — www.antiquariando.com

Be Modern — www.bemodern.net
Capperi — www.capperidicasa.com
Compendio Gallery — www.compendiogallery.com
Danord — www.danord.it
Décade — www.decade-decade.it
Deco XX Secolo Milan — www.decoxxsecolo.ch
Edizioni Stile Libero — www.stilelibero.it
Erastudio Apartment-Gallery —
        www.erastudioapartmentgallery.com
Flair Florence — www.flair.it
Galleria Colombari — www.galleriacolombari.com
Galleria O. Roma — www.galleriao.net
Nero — www.nero-design.it
Retro — www.retrodesign.it
Retro4m — www.retro4m.com
Rita Fancsaly — www.ritafancsaly.com
Spazio 900 — www.spazio900.com
Spot Gallery — www.spotgallery.it
Uso Interno — www.usointerno.com
STILSPIEL — www.stilspiel.de
Works Berlin — www.worksberlin.com

JAPAN
Bellbet — www.bellbet.net
Brunch — www.brunchone.com
Building — www.building-td.com
Create Taste — www.createtaste.com
De Mode — www.demode-furniture.net
Globe Antiques — www.globe-antiques.com
Moodys x Junks — www.moody-s.net
Meister — www.meister-mag.co.jp
Mid-Century Modern — www.mid-centurymodern.com
Lewis — www.lewis-meguro.com
Pour Annick — www.pourannick.com
Shark Attack — www.sharkattack.jp

NORWAY
Modern Tribute — www.moderntribute.com
Utopia Retro Modern — www.utopiaretromodern.com

SPAIN
20th Designs — www.20thdesigns.com
Against — www.againstbcn.com
Bakelita — www.bakelita.com
Fins de Siecles — www.finsdesiecles-artdeco.com
Gotham — www.gotham-bcn.com
Indigo50 — www.indigo50.es
Modernario — www.modernario.es
Modulolab — www.modulolab.com
Objetology — www.objetology.eu
Portuondo — www.portuondo.com

THE NETHERLANDS
050 Design — www.050design.nl

17 Design — www.17design.nl
Art of Vintage — www.artofvintage.nl
BarbMama Design — www.barbmama.nl
Bom Design Furniture — www.bomdesignfurniture.nl
Contemporary Showroom —
        www.contemporary-showroom.com
De Compaen — www.decompaen.nl
De Machinekamer — www.demachinekamer.nl
De Vreugde Design and Collectables —
        www.devreugdedesign.com
Viking Moderna — www.vikingmoderna.ch
woxx.designobjekte — www.woxx.ch
Decenniadesign — www.decenniadesign.nl
Design Revisited — www.designrevisited.com
Destijds Design — www.destijdsdesign.nl
Flatland Design — www.flatlanddesign.nl
Gaudium — www.galeriegaudium.com
Howaboutout — www.howaboutout.net
Huysraedt Vintage Industrial & Design —
        www.huysraedt.nl
Judith Wolberink Gallery — www.judithwolberink.com
Kameleon-Design — www.kameleon-design.nl
MARIEKKE vintage — www.mariekke.nl
Mass Modern Design — www.massmoderndesign.com
MD — www.midcenturydutch.com
Modern Design Gallery — www.moderndesigngallery.nl
Modern Vintage — www.modernvintage.nl
MooieStukken.nl — www.mooiestukken.nl
MORENTZ — www.morentz.com
Novac Vintage — www.novac-vintage.nl
Palissander — www.palissander.nl
Retro Revolution — www.retrorevolution.nl
Salonfähig — www.salonfahig.nl
Seventies design — www.seventiesdesign.nl
Stoelenwinkel — www.stoelenwinkel.nl
Studio1900 — www.studio1900.nl
Tante Eef Design — www.tanteeefdesign.nl
Tolve Art & Design — www.tolve.eu
Vaen Vintage Design Shop — www.vaenonline.nl
Van Ons — www.vanons.eu
Vintage Studio — www.vintage-studio.nl
Visavu Design — www.visavu.nl
Zo Goed Als Oud — www.zogoedalsoud.nl
Ztijl.nl — www.ztijl.com

SWEDEN
Bebop Antik — www.bebop.se
Edgeegg Form — www.edgeeggform.se
Jacksons — www.jacksons.se
Moderna Möbelklassiker —
        www.modernamobelklassiker.com
Modernity — www.modernity.se
Nirvanafurniture — www.nirvanafurniture.com
Nordisk Möbelkonst — www.nordiskmobelkonst.se
Nordlings — www.nordlingsantik.se

Retro Modern Design — www.retromoderndesign.com
Retroaktiv Design — www.retroaktivdesign.se
Schalling Modern Furniture Studio — www.schalling.se
Sjöström Antik — www.sjostromantik.se
Studio Carina Grefmar — www.studiocarinagrefmar.se
Sweden Antique — www.swedenantique.se
Wigerdals Värld — www.wigerdal.com
Yoni Store — www.yoni.se
Zimmerdahl 20th Century Design — www.zimmerdahl.se

SWITZERLAND
Bogen33 — www.bogen33.ch
Buma Design — www.bumadesign.ch
CH Design Furniture — www.chdesignfurniture.ch
demosmobilia DESIGN GALLERY —
        www.demosmobilia.ch
Design+Design — www.designunddesign.ch
Designbutik — www.designbutik.ch
designersdesign — www.designersdesign.ch
elastique — www.elastique.ch
EspaceModerne — www.espacemoderne.com
Galerie Kissthedesign — www.kissthedesign.ch
Galerie P! — www.jeanneret-chandigarh.com
Galerie Patrick Gutknecht —
        www.gutknecht-gallery.com
Individum — www.individum.ch
kokoska design — www.kokoska-design.ch
Les Illuminés Vintage Design XXE —
        www.lesilluminesdesign.ch
Lieblingsstuhl — www.lieblingsstuhl.ch
Monopol Design Antiquitäten — www.monopoldesign.ch
Okay Art — www.okayart.com
PPs Vintage Design — www.pps-vintagedesign.ch
Rock Objekte — www.rrock.ch
SUB Schönes & Besonderes —
        www.schoenesundbesonderes.ch
temporary addorisio — www.temporary-addorisio.ch
Timetunnel Living — www.timetunnel.ch

UNITED STATES
Almond Hartzog — www.almondhartzog.com
Christopher Anthony — www.christopheranthonyltd.com
Danish Modern Noho — www.danishmodernnoho.com
Demisch Danant — www.demischdanant.com
Brooklyn Mid-century Modern — www.brooklynmcm.com
Chris Houston Modern Artifacts —
        www.modernartifacts.net
Den Møbler — www.denmobler.com
District Modern — www.districtmodernlb.com
Donzella — www.donzella.com
Funkis Inc — www.funkisinc.com
Hammersby — www.hammersby.com
Hedge — www.hedgepalmsprings.com
Hostler Burrows — www.hostlerburrows.com
Machine Age — www.machine-age.com

Mid Century Maddist — www.midcenturymaddist.com
Mid Century Møbler — www.midcenturymobler.com
Mid-Century Modern Finds —
        www.midcenturymodernfinds.com
Mid-Century Modern Unique —
        www.midcenturymodernunique.com
MidcenturyLa — www.midcenturyla.com
Moderne Gallery — www.modernegallery.com
Patrick Parrish — www.patrickparrish.com
Pierre Anthony Galleries —
        www.pierreanthonygalleries.com
PS Modern Way — www.psmodernway.com
R & Company — www.r-and-company.com
Red Modern Furniture — www.redmodernfurniture.com
Reside — www.resideinc.com
Retro Passion 21 — www.retropassion21.com
Simply Mod — www.simplymod.com
Spaces — www.modern-spaces.net
Tomorrow's HousE — www.tomorrowshouse.info
Van der Most Modern — www.vandermostmodern.com
Venturaps — www.venturaps.com
Vintage Oasis — www.vintageoasis.com

AUCTIONS
Anderson and Garland Auctioneers —
        www.andersonandgarland.com
Annmaris — www.annmaris.fi
Auctionet — www.auctionet.com
Austin Auction Gallery — www.austinauction.com
Bonhams — www.bonhams.com
Botterweg Auctions Amsterdam — www.botterweg.com
Bruun Rasmussen Auctioneers —
        www.bruun-rasmussen.dk
Bukowskis — www.bukowskis.com
Chiswick Auctions — www.chiswickauctions.co.uk
Christie's — www.christies.com
Colombos — www.colombos.eu
Dorotheum — www.dorotheum.com
Drouot — www.drouot.com
Hagelstam & Co — www.hagelstam.fi
LAMA Los Angeles Modern Auctions —
        www.lamodern.com
Lauritz.com — www.lauritz.com
Phillips — www.phillips.com
Quittenbaum — www.quittenbaum.de
Rago Arts and Auctions — www.ragoarts.com Roseberys
        www.roseberys.co.uk
Skinner — www.skinnerinc.com
Sotheby's — www.sothebys.com
Svendborg Auktionerne — www.svendborg-auktionerne.dk
Sworders Fine Art Auctioneers — www.sworder.co.uk
Tajan — www.tajan.com
The Cabinet Rooms — www.thecabinetrooms.com
the saleroom — www.the-saleroom.com
Wright — www.wright20.com

FAIRS AND EVENTS
20th Century Cincinnati —
        www.20thcenturycincinnati.com
50er-70er Design Markt — www.design50er-70er.de
Antica Namur — www.antica.be
Antikmässan — www.antikmassan.se
Antiques + Modernism Winnetka —
        www.thewinnetkashow.com
Art Élysées — Art & Design — www.artelysees.fr
BRAFA Art Fair Brussels — www.brafa.be
Brussels Design Market —
        www.designseptember.be/designmarket/
Collective Design New York —
        www.collectivedesignfair.com
Design Classic düsseldorf — www.designclassic.de
Design Icons — www.design-icons.com
Design Markt Ghent — www.designmarkt.be
Design Miami/ — www.designmiami.com
design.Börse Berlin — www.design-boerse-berlin.de
Dubieus Design — www.dubieusdesign.be
Eurantica Brussels Fine Art Fair — www.eurantica.be
Fine Art Cologne — www.colognefineart.com
International Art Deco & Design Fair The Netherlands —
        www.nadb.nl
LA 20/21 Los Angeles Modern Design Show & Sale —
        www.lamodernism.com
Les Puces Du Design Paris — www.pucesdudesign.com
Les Puces Du Design Switzerland —
        www.pucesdudesign.ch
Midcentury East — www.modernshows.com
Midcentury Modern — www.modernshows.com
Midcentury South — www.modernshows.com
Modernism Week — www.modernismweek.com
New York 20th Century Art and Design Fair —
        www.dolphinfairs.com/nyc20/
Olympia International Art & Antiques Fair —
        www.olympia-antiques.com
PAD Art and Design — www.pad-fairs.com
Palm Springs Modernism —
        www.spring.palmspringsmodernism.com
Pan Amsterdam — www.pan.nl
Pier Antique Show — www.pierantiqueshow.com
Salon Du Vintage — www.salonduvintage.com
The Decorative Antiques and Textile Fair —
        www.decorativefair.com
The Salon Art+Design New York —
        www.thesalonny.com
TEFAF Maastricht — www.tefaf.com

Notes

1 Andrew Hollingsworth, *Danish Modern*, (Layton, 2008), p.38.

2 Paul Righini, *Thinking Architecturally: An Introduction to the Creation of Form and Place*, (Cape Town, 1999), p.101.

3 Entry for the Wassily Chair, 1925 on The Knoll Timeline, http://www.knoll.com/discover-knoll/timeline

4 Eames Demetrios, *Eames: Beautiful Details*, (Los Angeles, 2012).

5 Demetrios, *Eames: Beautiful Details*.

6 Demetrios, *Eames: Beautiful Details*.

7 From a summary of the chair on the Smithsonian website https://collection.cooperhewitt.org/objects/18714213/justification

8 Lauris Morgan-Griffiths, 'Honest, pure, functional, innovative', *Financial Times*, (8 July 2006).

9 From a biography of the designer on the Bruno Mathsson International website http://www.mathsson.se/en/about-bruno-mathsson-en

10 Ingrid Böhn-Jullander, *Bruno Mathsson*, (Lund, 1992), p. 296.

11 From the DUX website http://dux.com/About-DUX/DUX-by-Bruno-Mathsson/

12 From the Conran Shop website http://www.conranshop.co.uk/blue-tolix-a-chair.html

13 From the Tolix webpage http://facetoface.tolix.fr/en/home/chaise-a

14 From the blog of La Boutique Vintage http://www.laboutiquevintage.co.uk/blog/recognize-tolix-chairs-xavier-pauchard/

15 Ida van Zijl, *Gerrit Rietveld*, (London, 2010).

16 van Zijl, *Gerrit Rietveld*.

17 Penelope Rowlands, '100 Years After his Birth, New Life for Jean Prouvé', the *New York Times*, (11 April 2002) http://www.nytimes.com/2002/04/11/garden/100-years-after-his-birth-new-life-for-jean-prouve.html

18 Alistair Grieve, *Isokon, For Ease, For Ever* (London, 2004).

19 Grieve, *Isokon*.

20 Albert Pfeiffer, Knoll Museum curator, *Chicago Tribune*, (21 February 1999).

21 Jacques Barsac, *Charlotte Perriand: Complete Works Volume 2 1940–1955*, (Chicago, 2015).

22 Soren Hansen, 'Fremsynet enegænger sørgede for danske stole i USA', *Politiken*, (4 January 2010). http://politiken.dk/kultur/boger/faglitteratur_boger/article868935.ece

23 From a Finn Juhl biography on the R & Company website http://www.r-and-company.com/biography_detail.cfm?designer_id=69

24 Mira Nakashima, *Nature, Form and Spirit: The Life and Legacy of George Nakashima*, (New York, 2003).

25 Christian Holmsted Olesen, *Wegner: Just One Good Chair*, (Ostfildern, 2014), p. 99.

26 Hollingsworth, *Danish Modern*.

27 Anne Blond, ed., *Hans J. Wegner – A Nordic Design Icon from Tønder*, (Tønder, 2014).

28 Mike Rømer, *Finn Juhl and Onecollection*, (Stadil, 2013).

29 Poul Pilgaard Johnsen, 'Flirtatious Furniture', *The Attachment, 1*, (2008).

30 E30 'LCW Design of the Century', *Time* magazine, (31 December, 1999)

31 MOMA's director of Industrial Design, Eliot Noyes, quoted on the Eames Office website http://www.eamesoffice.com/the-work/dcw-2/

32 Charles and Ray Eames, *An Eames Anthology: Articles, Film Scripts, Interviews, Letters, Notes, and Speeches*, ed. Daniel Ostroff, (New Haven, 2015).

33 Brian Lutz, *Eero Saarinen: Furniture For Everyman*, (New York, 2012).

34 Eero Saarinen quoted in a collection entry on the MOMA website http://www.moma.org/collection/works/3639

35 From an interview with Marianne Wegner by the author.

36 Holmsted Olesen, *Wegner: Just One Good Chair*, p. 99.

37 Knorr quoted on the Knoll website http://www.knoll.com/designer/Don-Knorr

38 Wormley quoted on the Houston Museum of Fine Arts website http://www.mfah.org/research/archives/wormley-slide-archive/

39 From dealer Patrick Parrish's website http://www.patrickparrish.com/vintage/collection/seating/item/25

40 Carla Hartman and Eames Demetrios, (eds), *100 Quotes by Charles Eames*, (Los Angeles, 2007).

41 Ray Eames quoted in relation to a past exhibition at the Library of Congress http://www.loc.gov/exhibits/eames/furniture.html

42 From an interview with Hans Henrik Sørensen by the author.

43 Hans Henrik Sørensen interview.

44 Finn Juhl quoted on the Designers Revolt blog, The Revolutionary, http://revolt76.rssing.com/browser.php?indx=9942186&item=23

45 From an interview with Marianne Wegner by the author.

46 Jens Bernsen, *Hans J. Wegner*, (Copenhagen, 1994).

47 Hans J. Wegner quoted in the PP Møbler catalogue, (2015).

48 www.danish-design.com/designers/weg/#

49 From an interview with Marianne Wegner by the author.

50 Marianne Wegner interview.

51 Marianne Wegner interview.

52 Marianne Wegner interview.

53 Anne Blond (ed.), *Hans J. Wegner – A Nordic Design Icon from Tønder*, (Tønder, 2014).

54 From an interview with Paula Day by the author.

55 Alison Smithson, 'And Now The Dharmas Are Dying Out In Japan', *Architectural Design*, (September 1966).

56 http://www.theresidentssf.com/marco-zanuso/

57 www.fritzhansen.com

58 Arne Jacobsen quoted on the Jacobsen website http://www.arne-jacobsen.com/en/arne-jacobsen/designs

59 From an interview with Celia Bertoia by the author.

60 From an interview with Celia Bertoia by the author.

61 Celia Bertoia, *The Life and Work of Harry Bertoia: the Man, the Artist, the Visionary*, (Atglen, 2015).

62 Paula Day interview.

63 Charlotte and Peter Fiell, *Domus 1950–1959*, (Cologne, 2015), p.7.

64 Charles France quoted on collector and dealer

MCM Interior's website http://mcm-interiors.
blogspot.co.uk/p/france-son-furniture.html

65 Holmsted Olesen, *Wegner: Just One Good Chair*, p.87.

66 George Nelson quoted on the website seanmillsartist.
com/too\ededucation/nodes/11.html

67 Charles Eames quoted on Herman Miller website http://
www.hermanmiller.com/products/seating/lounge-
seating/eames-lounge-chair-and-ottoman.html

68 Peter Hall, 'Charles and Ray's Timeless Take',
Metropolis magazine, (June 2006) http://www.
metropolismag.com/June-2006/Charles-and-
Ray-rsquos-Timeless-Take/

69 Charles Eames quoted on the Eames Office website
http://www.eamesoffice.com/the-work/670-lounge-
chair671-ottoman/

70 Bradley Downs, owner of www.odd2mod.com, writes in
http://www.worthpoint.com/blog-entry/telling-age-
vintage-or-newer

71 Daniel Ostroff (ed.), *An Eames Anthology* (Yale 2015).

72 Axel Thygesen and Arne Karlsen, 'En Samtale med
Poul Kjærholm' and 'Mennesker og materialer',
Spatium magazine, (1963), pp.24–9.

73 Jørn Utzon quoted on the Designers Revolt blog,
The Revolutionary http://blog.designersrevolt.com/
post/61570013681/poul-kjaerholm-the-man-of-
steel

74 Poul Kjærholm quoted on the Skandium blog
https://www.skandium.com/blog/archives/2502

75 George Nelson quoted in the catalogue for the
exhibition 'George Nelson: Architecture, Writer,
Designer, Teacher' at the Vitra Design Museum,
(2012¬–13) https://designpracticesandparadigms.
files.wordpress.com/2013/01/wk6_george-nelson_
architect-writer-designer-teacher.pdf

76 Eeva Liisa Pelkonen and Donald Albrecht, *Eero
Saarinen: Shaping the Future*, (New Haven, 2011).

77 Amelia Gentleman, 'A City That Sat on Its Treasures,
but Didn't See Them', the *New York Times*, (19 March
2008) http://www.nytimes.com/2008/03/19/world/
asia/19chandigarh.html

78 Gio Ponti, 'Senza aggetivi', *Domus 268* (March 1952).

79 From an interview with Simon Andrews at Christie's,
London, by the author.

80 From an interview with Benjamin Cherner by the author.

81 Poul Erik Tøjner, *Arne Jacobsen: Architect & Designer*,
(Danish Design Center 1994).

82 Arne Jacobsen quoted on www.arne-jacobsen.com

83 From an interview with Dennie Ditzel by the author.

84 Alexandra Lange, 'The Mother of Us All', Design
Observer website, (5 November 2012) http://
designobserver.com/feature/the-mother-of-us-
all/34158/

85 Daniel Ostroff (ed.), *An Eames Anthology* (Yale 2015).

86 Élisabeth Vedrenne and Anne-Marie Fèvre, *Pierre
Paulin*, (Paris, 2001), quotation translated from
the French.

87 Pierre Perrone, obituary of Pierre Paulin, the
Independent (5 August 2009) http://www.
independent.co.uk/news/obituaries/pierre-paulin-
innovative-designer-who-helped-to-revolutionise-
everyday-furniture-1767749.html

88 Anya Lawrence, 'Remembering Pierre Paulin', *Disegno*,
(30 September 2015) http://www.disegnodaily.com/
article/ligne-rosett-edits-pierre-paulin

89 Verner Panton quoted on the website http://www.
verner-panton.com/person/biographie/9/

90 *Form* magazine No.46, (May 1969).

91 Rob Walker, 'The Guts of a New Machine', *New York
Times* magazine (30 November 2003).

92 Pilar Viladas, 'Modern Man', the *New York Times*
(4 December 2005). http://www.nytimes.
com/2005/12/04/style/tmagazine/modern-man.html

93 Phil Patton, 'Public Eye; 30 Years after *Space Odyssey*,
the *New York Times* (19 February 1998).

94 From an interview with Eero Aarnio on Euromaxx
for Deutsche Welle https://www.youtube.com/
watch?v=MJNMknukN0w

95 Quoted in the Eero Aarnio biography on the Herman
Miller website http://www.hermanmiller.com/
designers/aarnio.html

96 Charles Pollock quoted on the Knoll website http://
www.knoll.com/knollnewsdetail/reintroducing-657-
arm-chair-charles-pollock

97 http://icandigthis.com/shop/7lbbuom96bmvfqjattpcn
g7373s5t4

98 Perrone, Paulin obituary, the *Independent* (5 August
2009).

99 From an interview with Pierre Paulin at the

Maison & Objet Design Fair, Paris, on Möbel
Kultur Kanal (2008) https://www.youtube.com/
watch?v=6YaY2vl0XhQ

100 From an article about the Kartell Museum on the
designboom website (12 April 2015) http://www.
designboom.com/design/kartell-museo-04-12-2015/

101 Dirk Limburg, interview with Martin Visser, NRC, (11
August 2006) http://vorige.nrc.nl/article1710365.ece

102 Petra Starink, 'Martin Visser: Collector, Designer,
Free Spirit', *ArchitectuurNL* (13 March 2012)
http://www.architectuur.nl/nieuws/martin-visser-
verzamelaar-ontwerper/

103 Walter Platner quoted on the Knoll website www.knoll.
com/product/platner-lounge-chair

104 From an interview with Felix Ghyczy by the author.

105 Gaetano Pesce quoted on the Design Museum website
https://designmuseum.org/design/chairs-1960s

106 Teresa Cannatà, 'Gaetano Pesce', *Vogue* Italia
(15 April 2011) http://www.vogue.it/en/people-
are-talking-about/focus-on/2011/04/gaetano-
pesce#sthash.03z2BiHe.dpuf

107 From an interview with Rodney Kinsman by the author.

108 From an interview with Barbara Radice by the author.

109 From an Ettore Sottsass biography on the R &
Company website http://www.r-and-company.com/
biography_detail.cfm?designer_id=104

110 Barbara Isenberg, *Conversations with Frank Gehry*,
(New York, 2009).

Index

First published in the United Kingdom in 2016 by Pavilion
An imprint of HarperCollins*Publishers*
1 London Bridge Street
London SE1 9GF

www.harpercollins.co.uk

HarperCollins*Publishers*
Macken House
39/40 Mayor Street Upper
Dublin 1
D01 C9W8
Ireland

ISBN 978-1-910904-33-6

A CIP catalogue record for this book is available from the British Library.

10 9 8 7 6 5 4 3 2

Reproduction by Rival
Printed and bound in China by RR Donnelley APS

Cover illustration © Hyperkit

This book is produced from independently certified FSC™ paper to ensure responsible forest management.

For more information visit: www.harpercollins.co.uk/green